ANTONIO BERNARDO

Bernadette

recounts her apparitions

Editions Doucet
65100 LOURDES

Introduction

Much has been written and recounted about the apparitions in Lourdes. However, the most authentic and vivid account has been left to us by Bernadette herself. It is an account without any distortion, an account which is essentially characterized by its simplicity, fluency, liveliness and spontaneity. It is as simple and spontaneous as Bernadette always showed herself to be.

Complete and detailed narratives of great value have been written about the events which took place in Lourdes through the witnesses and documents of that time, although all of them have drawn from the accounts of Saint Bernadette herself.

Bernadette's accounts are all different but in their entirety they represent the most genuine evidence of the apparitions. The present publication aims at introducing them to the reader in the way that Bernadette left them to us.

The accounts are preceded by a concise description of the life of the Saint; as much as is necessary to allow the reader to understand all the tragedy of poverty, suffering, incomprehension and humiliation which characterized the life of this young girl priviliged by Our Lady; as much as is necessary to make us love this Saint, even if there were still any need to do so.

This publication also contains a reproduction of the autographed manuscript on the apparitions, photographs of the main protagonists connected with the events, and other photos concerning the Sanctuary of Lourdes. The work as a whole constitutes not only a work of enthralling interest to the reader, but also an indispensable record for the pilgrim.

The Author

◂ *BERNADETTE SOUBIROUS*
(Lourdes 7-1-1844 - Nevers 16-4-1879)

Here is Bernadette

Who was Bernadette? She was the daughter of a miller reduced to poverty. A simple young shepherdess, submissive to her nurse in Bartrès.

An unappreciated religious girl, humbled and submissive in the convent of Nevers. A girl who consciously and generously spent her short life in suffering.

Above all, Bernadette is a disturbing witness to and messenger of Mary Immaculate to people of every period.

7th January 1844

Bernadette is born at the mill of Boly to the married couple François Soubirous and Louise Castèrot. On 9th January she is christened Marie Bernarde at the parish church of Lourdes, St. Peter's. Her godfather and godmother are Jean Védère and her aunt Bernarde Castèrot.

November 1844

Bernadette is about 10 months old. Her mother loses her milk because of an accident and can no longer breast-feed her child. Bernadette is entrusted to the care of a wet nurse in Bartrès: she is Marie Lagues, a friend of Louise's, who had lost her son Jean at the time of his birth.

1st April 1846

Bernadette is now 26 months old. It is the age of weaning. She comes back to her parents at the mill of Boly and remains there until the 24th June 1854, the date on which François Soubirous finally leaves the mill, thus embarking on the tragedy of poverty and suffering which will lead him to the dungeon.

Autumn 1855

In Lourdes the plague breaks out. Bernadette is eleven and she is affected by it. Her sores are treated in a rudimentary way. Repeated friction with rags of straw expose her sores in order to eliminate the cancerous parts and dress them.

Thanks to this very painful, though effective, remedy Bernadette recovers, but she gets asthma from which she will suffer for the rest of her life. Indeed, it will soon be compounded by tuberculosis of the bones of her legs. And it will be a combination of asthma and tuberculosis which will lead her to the grave at the age of 35.

Maison Paternelle (Bernadette's father's house).

November 1856

François is reduced to the direst poverty. He is without a permanent job, without a home, with a wife and four children to look after. He takes lodgings as best he can in the Cachot (the dungeon), a damp and unhealthy room in a former prison lent by his cousin André Sajous.

Bernadette is thirteen and shares the same destiny as her family.

September 1857

Bernadette goes back to Bartrès to her nurse Marie Langues. The latter needs help and is looking for someone who is able to do everything: to tend the flock, to carry out the work of the home and, above all, to look after little Jean who is only two years old.

Life in Bartrès is hard for Bernadette under every circumstance. In this atmosphere of toil, adversity and sacrifice she tries to learn the catechism in order to prepare herself for Holy Communion.

She finds it very difficult both because of the lack of time and on account of her very limited learning ability. The answer she one day gave to the parish priest in Bartrès is meaningful:

"It is easier for me to put the book of the catechism in my head than to learn the lesson".

21st January 1858

The atmosphere of hardship and sacrifice at Bartrès, her loneliness and the homesickness she feels for her family, and the wish to prepare herself with more calmness and better opportunity for Holy Commun-ion, induce Bernadette to go back to Lourdes. It is in fact, Thursday, 21st January.

In the dungeon she again finds poverty, dampness and the bad smell of a dark and narrow room. She again finds, however, the love of her parents and the company of Antoinette and her brothers.

11th February 1858

It is about eleven in the morning of the Thursday before Shrove Tuesday. The day is darkened by the thick, damp fog typical of Lourdes. In the cold and unhealthy dungeon there is no more wood.

Bernadette, her younger sister, Antoinette and their friend, Jeanne Abadie go to the area of Massabielle to make bundles of firewood and to pick up some bones to sell.

"...I heard a noise like a gust of wind... I raised my eyes towards the grotto and saw a lady dressed in white. She was wearing a white dress, a white veil, a blue girdle and a yellow rose on each foot."

It is the beginning of the apparitions. The special particular mission of Bernadette begins. Lourdes becomes a world centre of pilgrimage.

Soubirous's family. At the center of the photo: Bernadette with the white "capulet".

4th June 1858

"Yesterday" the 3th June, the feast of the Body and Blood of Christ, Bernadette received her First Communion in the chapel of the hospice. She seemed truly conscious and fully aware of the event. During the retreat of spiritual preparation her conduct, her concentration and her attention were really praiseworthy. Everything took place in her in a wonderful way! *(Letter of Fr. Peyramale to Mgr. Laurence).*

Bernadette is fourteen and a half years old.

11th February - 16th July 1858

It is the period in which the eighteen apparitions take place. Our Lady has on most occasions simply prayed with Bernadette and allowed herself to be contemplated. Other times she has spoken to her and given her instructions, thus bequeathing us the message and the spirituality of Lourdes.

15th July 1860

Bernadette is taken to the hospice of Lourdes because of yet another attack of asthma. She will remain there until her departure for the convent of Nevers in 1866.

*Boly Mill.
The room where
Bernadette
was born.*

*Bartrès,
the Bergerie
(sheepfold).
Here Bernadette,
the shepherdess,
brought the flock
of her nurse
after leading
them down
from pasture.*

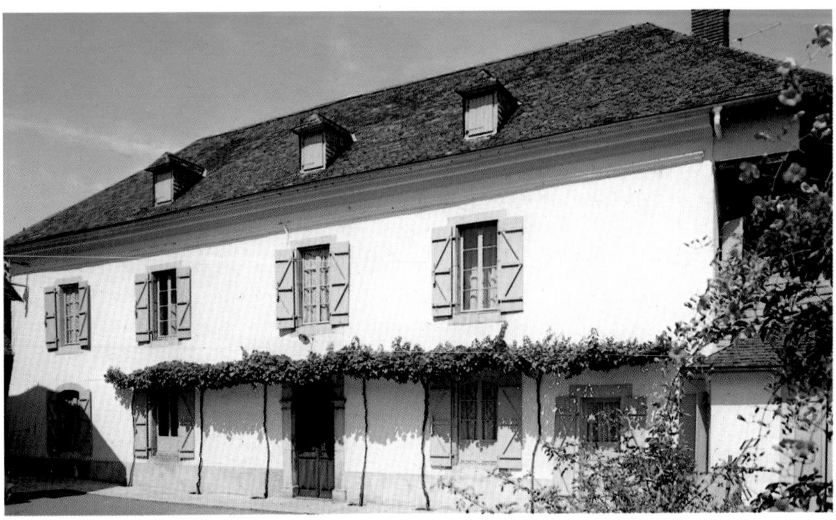

*Bartrès.
The Laguës home
where Bernadette
lived during
her stay with
the nurse.*

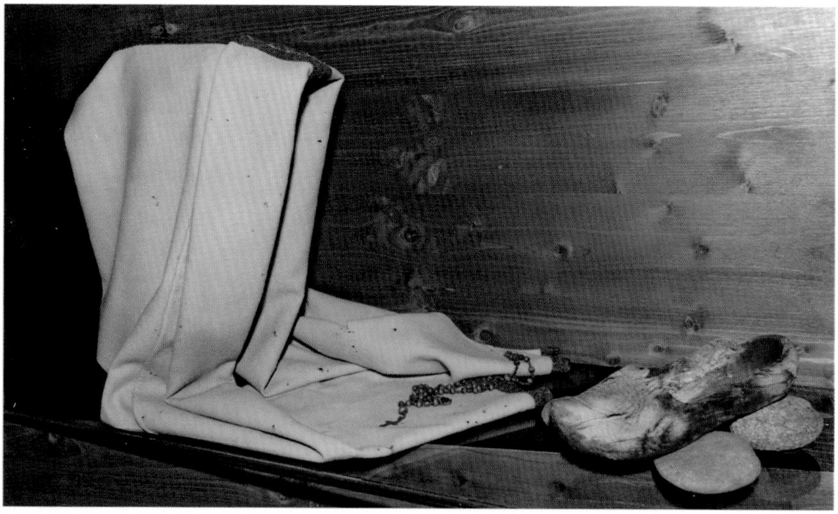

Le Cachot. The dwelling-place of the Soubirous's family at the time of the Apparitions.

19th May 1866

The crypt at Lourdes is inaugurated by Mgr. Laurence. It is the first concrete answer to the wish of Our Lady. "I wish a chapel to be built here". Bernadette is there.

Her departure for the convent has been deliberately postponed.

Statue of Mary Immaculate in gilt wood. At the time of the Apparitions it was situated in the parish church. Bernadette often prayed in front of it. Today it is at the Cachot (the dungeon).

3rd July 1866

Bernadette has for a long time serenely reflected on the direction her life should take. She has decided to become a nun. She chooses the Order of the Sisters of Charity in Nevers.

Before leaving for her novitiate in Nevers, she goes and visits, secretly and dressed as a nun, the holy grotto for the last time. She will never return there.

7th July 1866

Bernadette enters the convent of Saint Gildard. She finds great difficulty in getting used to the place.

30th October 1867

Bernadette takes her Religious Profession together with 43 other novices.

The ceremony takes place in the hall of the novitiate of the convent before Mgr. Forcade, Bishop of Nevers and the Mother Superior of the Order, Sister Imbert. To each nun a task and a goal is entrusted.

Bernadette remains in Nevers, because she is ill and is considered incapable. She is entrusted with the task of working in the infirmary of the convent and of helping in the kitchen.

28th March 1878

She is struck by another attack of asthma. She becomes worse and worse. First the Sacraments are administered to her; then Extreme Unction (for the fourth time since 1868).

On this occasion she makes the following humorous remark:

"Everytime you have administered Extreme Unction to me, I have recovered". This time, however, Bernadette will improve a little, but she will not recover.

The Grotto at the time of the Apparitions. (Original Photograph). ▸

The Crypt.

Hospice of Lourdes. The kneeler where Bernadette received her first communion.

Hospice of Lourdes. Here Bernadette made her first communion. Here she remained in 1860 and in 1866 for the cure of asthma.

The Museum of Nevers: the armchair in which Bernadette died on 16 April 1879 after yet another attack of asthma.

Bernadette with sister Alessandrine Roques, Superior of the hospice of Lourdes.
Photo taken on 19 May 1866.

The Crucifix of the Religious Profession of Bernadette placed in her coffin; and remains of the rosary placed in her hands in her coffin.

14th April 1879

Bernadette lies on her sick-bed. With her feeble voice almost broken by her difficulty in breathing she tells Sister Leontine: "I am ground like a grain wheat. I would never have imagined I would have to suffer so much!". The remark epitomises Bernadette's whole life of suffering.

16 April 1879

Again asthma attacks. Following the doctor's advice she is stretched out in an armchair in order to make her breathing easier. She dies at 3 p.m.. The asthma and the tuberculosis of the bones of her legs have wasted her away, thus leading her to the grave at the age of just over 35.

One day she summarised her whole life, her whole mission and message on a piece of paper:

"To obey is to love! To suffer in silence for Christ is joy! To love sincerely is to give everything, even grief!"

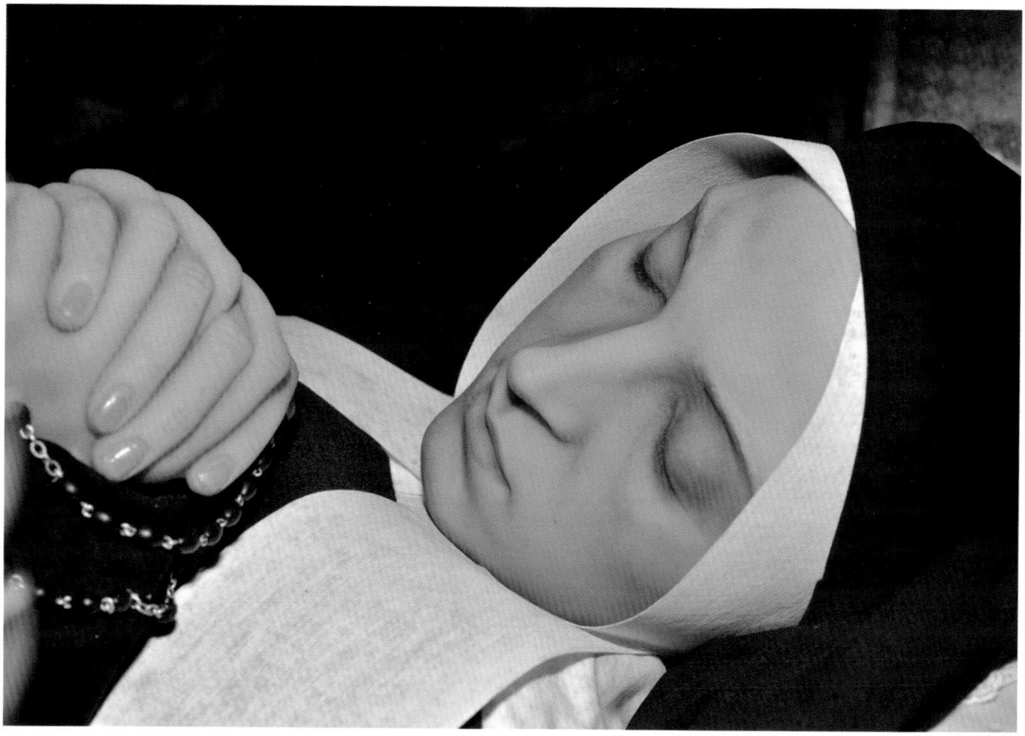

The body of Bernadette.

8th December 1933

It is the Feast of the Immaculate Conception. It is the Jubilee Year, instituted extraordinarily by Pope Pius XI to celebrate the Redemption. Pius XI himself proclaims Bernadette a Saint.

On the occasion of the recognition for the Canonical Process of Canonization, Bernadette's body has been found in a perfect state. Today, intact and covered by a very thin layer of wax for preservation, her body rests inside a bronze and crystal casket. In Lourdes Bernadette remains close to the sick and the handicapped in the chapel of the convent of Nevers with the message of her suffering lived in hope and joy. She remains close to the pilgrim with the evidence of her life and with the message of Our Lady.

The accounts of the Appartions

Many times Bernadette recounted the events in Massabielle before the civil and ecclesiastical authorities, in reply to the numerous and increasing pressures of her friends, priests and pilgrims, all of them eager to hear from her personally what had really happened in the grotto. What are we in possession of today regarding these accounts? First of all, the narration of the apparitions on the part of Bernadette must be divided into two parts: the oral and the written. The first category is comprised by: the deposition on **21st February 1858** before the Head of the Police in Lourdes;

- that on **17th November 1858** before the diocesan subcommittee of inquiry;
- that on **7th December 1860** before the Bishop of Tarbes-Lourdes, Mgr. Laurence and the diocesan commission.
- Finally Bernadette's "declaration" on **13 October 1865** to the journalist Henri Lassere and signed by her.

As regards the written accounts, Bernadette's autographed narratives are of particular importance. We list them in chronological order as follows:

- Narrative of **28th May 1862**. It consists of a letter addressed to Father Gondrand. It is the first autographed manuscript in order of time we know in this connection.
- Narrative of **22nd August 1864**. It consists of a letter addressed to the Abbé Charles Bouin. It is in effect a synthesis of the preceeding narrative.
- Narrative of **20th November 1865**. Letter addressed to an unknown lady through Ida Ribettes. Such a letter never reached the addressee. It contains only the words addressed by the Virgin to Bernadette.
- Narrative added to the two pages of the letter addressed to the unknown lady. The date is uncertain. It is the general opinion that it was written on 20th November 1865 to complete the short letter.
- The **"Grotte de Lourdes"** in 1866. This consists of three narratives in rough copy. According to Bernadette's wishes they should serve as the basis for a definitive and accurate draft of the events in Massabielle to take with her to Nevers. This account contains many erasures and corrections, but it is the most detailed and complete account of those that are known.

"The Carnet à la Reine du Ciel" on 12th May 1866. It is an account written in a personal note-book and mostly copied from the preceding "Grotte de Lourdes".

To these accounts a precious manuscript can be added: **"The Words of the Apparition"** in Bigourdan dialect. Bernadette wrote them herself on **24th April 1865**, on the back of an image of St. John Berchmans at the request of Father Cros. It is the only autographed transcription of the words of the Virgin that is known to us.

Style and evaluation

What can be said about Bernadette's narratives in general and about the autographed ones in particular? They have the characteristic of being simple, fluent and spontaneous in description. As regards the autographed accounts, the style is in incorrect and local French dialect. Bernadette was concerned about the description of the event, but not about the style.

Besides, one must not forget her cultural and social condition. Daughter of a humble miller, she had spent her infancy in illiteracy. She had begun school only a few years before.

The subject. On 30th January 1879 Mother Dons replied by letter to Father Cros in the name of Bernadette as follows:

"Sister Marie-Bernarde vouches that her (Bernadette's) account of the apparitions is substantially correct. No account should therefore be taken of the chronology of the events, since she herself knew neither what date nor what day it was at the time of their occurrence."

This statement, 13-14 years later than the manuscript, gives a precise evaluation of their content. Bernadette mentions some dates and days which effectively correspond, but she has put the most salient facts in writing as she remembered them at the time of the draft. Consequently, the autographed narratives must be considered as a whole and above all in relation to the witnesses and the documents of that time.

Even though written in incorrect, local French dialect and although fragmentary and without any chronological order, they represent as a whole the most genuine evidence for the apparitions. A complete and detailed reconstruction of the events in Lourdes has been achieved through the witnesses, depositions and documents of that time, but always and above all on the basis of Bernadette's own narratives. In these documents, taken as a whole, a disproportion can be noted between the account of the first two apparitions and the others; above all from the third one to that on 25th March, disproportion in the length of the texts and in the distinctness of the mem-

VIRON
LOURDES

ories. Disproportion in the order of the events, in their chronological exactness, in the abundance of the details etc.. In spite of its conciseness and the lack of a precise chronology of the events, the third apparition is dominated by four particulars: the Lady asks Bernadette to return fifteen times to the grotto, to go and tell the priests to build a chapel on the spot where the apparitions appeared, to drink at the fountain and wash herself, and to pray for sinners.

In spite of this we know for certain that the four requests occurred on the occasion of different apparitions.

How can we explain this chronological unification of the four requests? In my opinion, as the years went by and owing to the consciousness of her mission, in Bernadette's mind and memory there formed three different pictures of the events, each of them with a precise meaning quite apart from the chronology of the facts. A picture of silent apparitions and of contemplation.

Firstly, **the Lady introduces herself**; then the events, the circumstances, the name of the persons moving around the apparitions are more emphasized.

Secondly, **the Lady speaks.** It is the third apparition with the request of the fifteen meetings It represents a picture of confidences, of missions rather than of contemplation.

Thirdly, finally **the Lady reveals herself: "I am the Immaculate Conception".** It is a picture of closure-contemplation. It is the authentication of a message and of a mission. This kind of "forma mentis" in Bernadette has been the constant guiding thread of her narratives.

The Commissioner Jacomet

"…I was led before the Commissioner of Police. He received me in a room in which he was alone… He took a sheet of paper and told me to tell him what had happened at the grotto."

Domenique Jacomet *was born on 17th October 1821 in Argelès. He died on 5th August 1873 in Paris. He was the Chief of Police in Lourdes from 1st November 1853 to the end of November 1858. He played a rôle of primary importance in the story of and in the decisions about the events of Lourdes. A person who was undoubtedly intelligent, capable, devoted to work. He was esteemed and enjoyed the full confidence both of the Prefect Massy and of the Prosecutor Dutour. He was their constant informant about the "case of Massabielle". His "Reports" and his advice were determining factors in the decisions and attitude of the other two.*

His own attitude towards Bernadette and the "case of Massabielle" was not only suspicious but often merciless and threatening. He followed her and kept her under constant surveillance, watching and waiting for the favourable occasion of a mistake on her part or an infringement of the law in order to draw the consequences. He was the first to interrogate Bernadette officially on 21st February and to draw up the report of the deposition on the events. He could not admit at all that a girl in such a social, cultural and religious condition as Bernadette could be the object of a supernatural event at the grotto of Massabielle. He was completely convinced that she was affected by hallucinations. Later the suspicion arose in him that she was being exploited by those who had an interest in the story of the apparitions. And the ever more evident proof of the supernatural events of Lourdes did not make him change his mind.

He was transferred at the end of November 1858 thanks to a promotion. He was present at the 15th apparition on 4th March, but for reasons of work. For the rest, in drawing up his "reports" he gathered news, listened to Bernadette and was constantly kept well informed by his police officials.

He took part in all the meetings held by the civil authorities in Lourdes as regards the case of Massabielle and he always supported the hard line in order to drastically curb the movement that had grown up around Bernadette and the apparitions. He received from the Prefect the order to close the grotto and see to it that the Prefect's ban on admission to the Massabiélle area was respected.

In the presence of the Commissioner Jacomet

(21-2-1858)

Bernadette's deposition before Jacomet about the events in Lourdes is the first written document we know in order of time. It exists in duplicate. Both of them drawn up by the Commissioner. Both of them without signature.

The first is a rough copy written as a first draft after the following up of Bernadette's story. It contains many erasures which bear witness to the various attempts and subterfuges used by Jacomet to confuse Bernadette and make her contradict herself.

The second copy, more extensive and detailed, is a successive draft reformulated, expanded and put into fair copy. In any case, it is faithful to the first draft. Jacomet lent this version to the Prosecutor Dutour who used it as an outline for the questioning of Bernadette on 25th February 1858.

The preface to the deposition does not exist in the rough copy, which begins with the first words pronounced by Bernadette. The two originals are preserved in the archives of the grotto of Lourdes. For reasons of completeness and of details we quote here only the second text with the corresponding preface.

Preamble of the Commissioner

"I, J. Domenique Jacomet, Commissioner of Police of the Canton of Lourdes (High Pyrenees), had been informed that a girl claimed to have been in contact with the Virgin who had appeared in a grotto called Massavielle [1] on the banks of the river on the outskirts of Lourdes and that in certain moments she fell into an ecstasy.

After a few days, the news circulated in the town, producing some agitation in simple and credulous people. For this reason, I had the girl brought into my presence. I asked her for her name and age, and asked her to tell me what she had seen.

I asked her to explain to me what she had experienced after the first apparition at the grotto and to tell me to whom she had confided these first revelations of hers. Her deposition is as follows."

Deposition of Bernadette

"My name is Bernadette Soubirous of Lourdes. I am 13-14 years old [2].

I can neither read nor write and I haven't yet taken my First Communion.

On 11 February, market day in Tarbes, Jeanne Baloume [3] came to fetch me so that we could go along the banks of the river together to collect bones.

Before crossing the canal of Madame Lafitte's mill to go across to

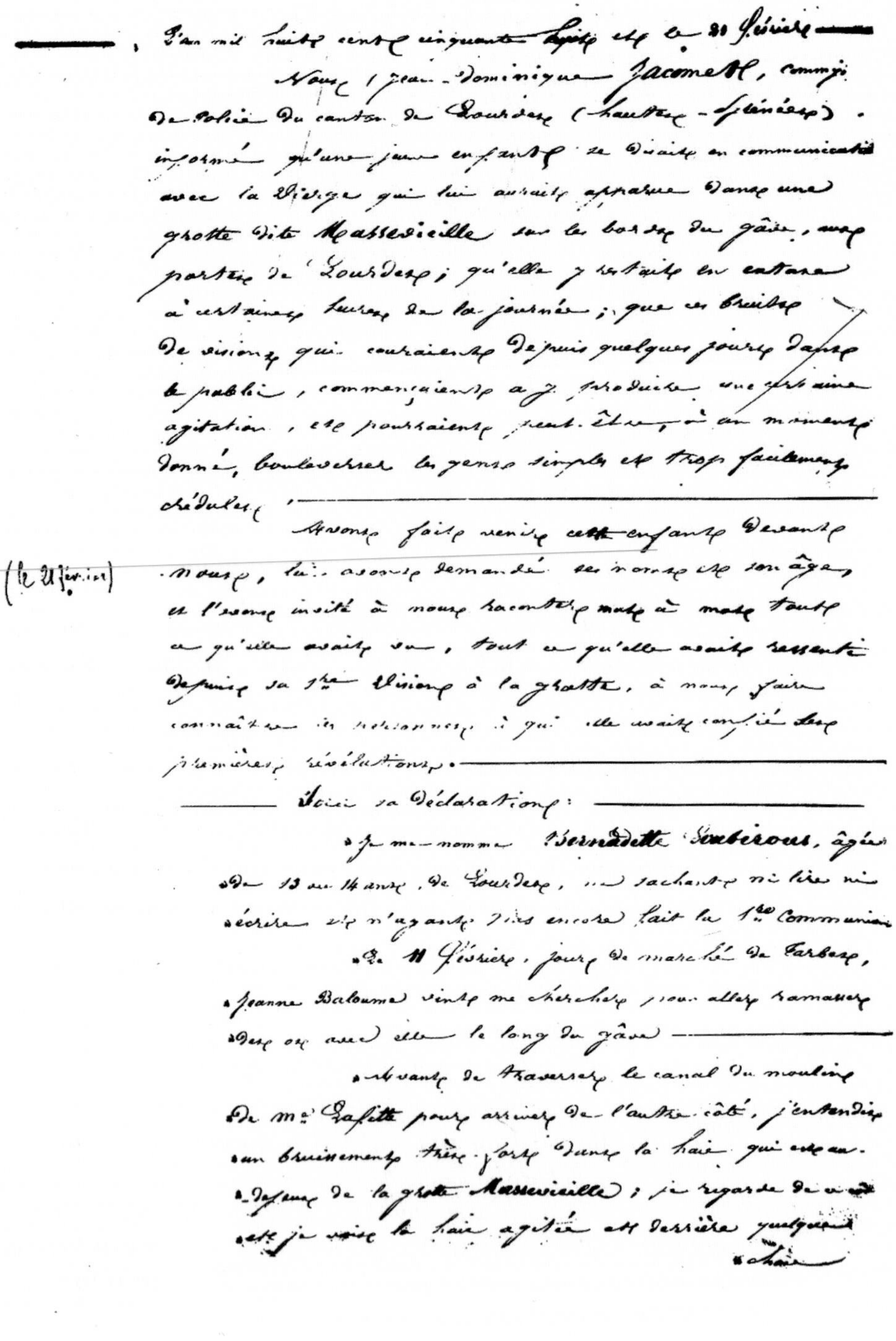
L'an mil huit cent cinquante huit et le 21 février

Nous, Jean-Dominique Jacomet, commissaire de police du canton de Lourdes (Hautes-Pyrénées), informé qu'une jeune enfant se disait en communication avec la Vierge qui lui aurait apparu dans une grotte dite Massevieille sur les bords du Gave, aux portes de Lourdes; qu'elle y restait en extase à certaines heures de la journée; que ces bruits de visions qui couraient depuis quelques jours dans le public, commençaient à y produire une certaine agitation, et pourraient peut-être, à un moment donné, bouleverser les gens simples et trop facilement crédules.

(le 21 février) Avons fait venir cette enfant devant nous, lui avons demandé ses noms et son âge, et l'avons invitée à nous raconter mot à mot tout ce qu'elle avait vu, tout ce qu'elle avait ressenti depuis sa 1re vision à la grotte, à nous faire connaître les personnes à qui elle avait confié ses premières révélations.

Voici sa déclaration:

« Je me nomme Bernadette Soubirous, âgée de 13 ou 14 ans, de Lourdes, ne sachant ni lire ni écrire et n'ayant pas encore fait la 1re Communion.

« Le 11 février, jour de marché de Tarbes, « Jeanne Baloume vint me chercher pour aller ramasser « des os avec elle le long du Gave.

« Avant de traverser le canal du moulin « de Mr Lafitte pour arriver de l'autre côté, j'entendis « un bruissement très fort dans la haie qui est au-« dessous de la grotte Massevieille; je regarde de ce côté « et je vois la haie agitée et derrière quelque

« chose

First page of the deposition of Bernadette before the Commissioner Jacomet.

the other side, I heard a very loud noise amid the shrubbery above the Massavielle grotto.

Looking in that direction, I noticed that the shrubbery was shaking a great deal and that there was something white behind it that resembled a girl.

I gazed at the apparition for an instant (4), then I fell on my knees and began to pray. **Aquerò** (5) smiled at me and then moved into the grotto.

In the meantine my companions were skipping about on the other bank of the canal. I asked them if they had seen something. They replied that they hadn't. They asked me what had happened. I answered: "Nothing important".

I began collecting wood together with my sister and Baloume' who left straight away. I was left alone with my 10-years old sister Marie and on the road back home I spoke to her about the apparition.

Around three o'clock in the afternoon I spoke about it at home. During dinner I also told my mother about it. She replied that it was surely a dream. In the evening I spoke about it with my aunt Romana who lives above us. She told me that it could only have been the effect of hallucination.

On Sunday, 14th February, after Mass, I returned to the grotto together with some of my friends. To be precise, with Jeanne Noguès, Justine Soubies, Marie Chouatou, Annette Sère and my sister Marie. We brought with us a small bottle of holy water which Justine Soubies and Marie Chouatou had taken from the church.

On arriving at the grotto, we knelt and began reciting the rosary. **Aquerò** once again appeared in the niche of the grotto.

Baloume came after us and remained somewhat at a distance. She stopped on the path through the woods and threw a stone from on top of the grotto which passed over our heads. Frightened, we ran away (6).

When I asked **Aquerò** whether she came from God or the devil, she had already vanished.

Before Vespers, Cuilhé-Geste came to my home and I spoke to her about the apparition. On Monday, 15th February, I spoke about it to the Superior of the hospice and to the Sister in charge of the sewing workshop. They told me to attach no importance to the matter, because it was the effect of hallucination.

On the morning of Tuesday 16th, Madame Milhet sent her granddaughter to call me. I refused to go. She again called me in the evening and this time I went. I told her everything. We agreed to go to the grotto together early next Sunday morning. She didn't have enough patience, however, to wait until the date we had agreed on. In fact, she came to fetch me at home together with Madame Peyret on Thursday morning, 18th February. It was very early and I was still in bed.

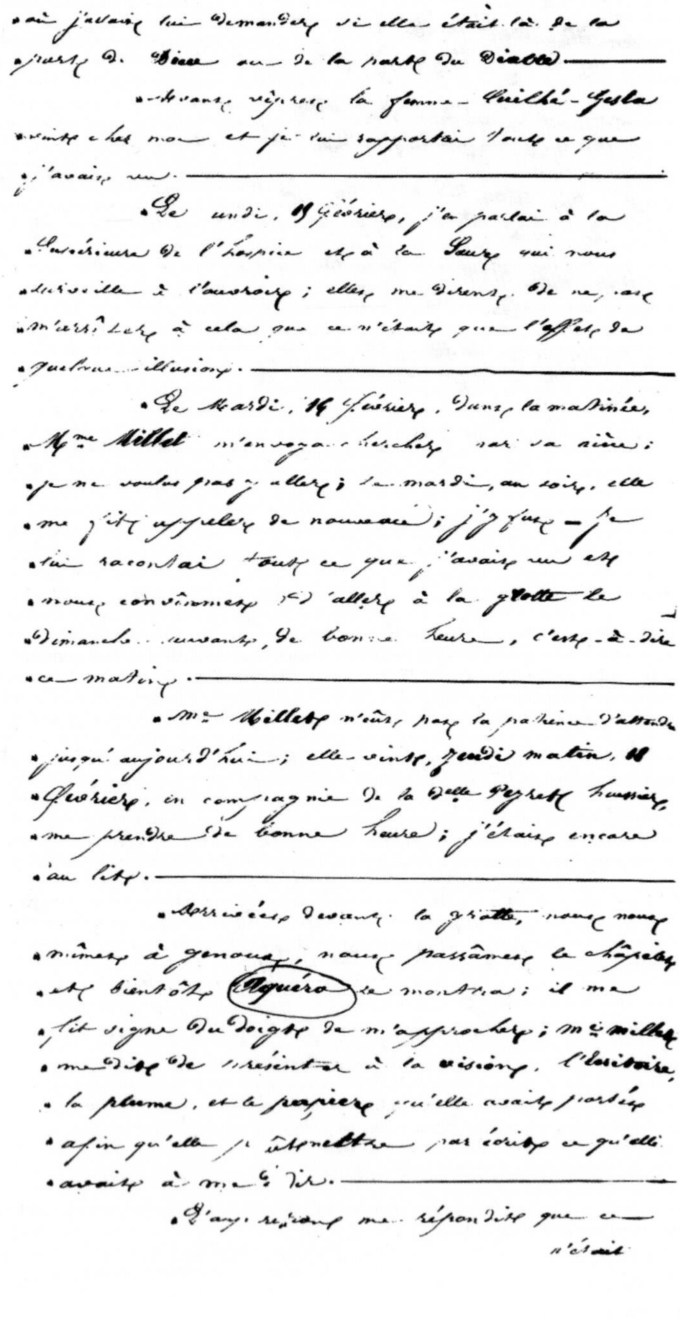
« où j'avais lui demandé si elle était là de la part de Dieu ou de la part du Diable. ——

« Avant vêpres, la femme Cuilhé-Gesla vint chez moi et je lui rapportai tout ce que j'avais vu. ——

« Le lundi, 15 février, j'en parlai à la Supérieure de l'hospice et à la Sœur qui nous surveille à l'ouvroir ; elles me dirent de ne pas m'arrêter à cela que ce n'était que l'effet de quelque illusion. ——

« Le Mardi, 16 février, dans la matinée, Mme Millet m'envoya chercher par sa bonne : je ne voulus pas y aller ; le mardi, au soir, elle me fit appeler de nouveau ; j'y fus — je lui racontai tout ce que j'avais vu et nous convînmes d'aller à la grotte le dimanche suivant, de bonne heure, c'est-à-dire le matin. ——

« Mme Millet n'eut pas la patience d'attendre jusqu'aujourd'hui ; elle vint, jeudi matin, 18 février, en compagnie de la Delle Peyret lingère, me prendre de bonne heure ; j'étais encore au lit. ——

« Arrivées devant la grotte, nous nous mîmes à genoux, nous passâmes le chapelet et bientôt Aquéro se montra ; il me fit signe du doigt de m'approcher ; Mme Millet me dit de présenter à la vision, l'écritoire, la plume, et le papier qu'elle avait portés afin qu'elle y mettrait par écrit ce qu'elle avait à me dire. ——

« L'aq. répons me répondit que ce n'était

Third page of the deposition. Clearly visible at the bottom is the dialect word Aquerò (= that one there) by which Bernadette called the apparition.

On reaching the grotto, we knelt and began reciting the rosary.

Aquerò appeared straight away and motioned me with her finger to draw near.

Madame Milhet asked me to present her with the paper, pen and ink well that she had brought with her and to ask her to put into writing what she wanted of me. The apparition replied to me that this was not necessary. She asked me to have the goodness to keep returning to the grotto for 15 days.

Madame Milhet also charged me to ask whether her presence were pleasing to her. **Aquerò** answered me that it was not excessively displeasing.

On the Thursday and Friday, respectively the 18th and 19th February, I had lunch, dinner and slept at the Milhets, home. Yesterday, on the other hand, I only had lunch and dinner there. I returned home in the evening because my aunt didn't want me to stay any longer with Madame Milhet".

NOTES

1) The word **Massavieille** had no fixed spelling. In other documents of that time we find it written in a different way. The spelling used by Jacomet was evidently the most common and best-known in Lourdes. Apart from the spelling, everyone in the village knew what the word **Massevieille** (=old rock) corresponded to. It gave the name to the entire low area of Lourdes, consisting prevalently of common woods and marshy little islands produced by the deviation and the overflowing of the river.

2) Bernadette was born on 7th January 1844. Therefore she was fourteen and not thirteen.

3) **BALOUME**: family nickname. Jeanne's surname was Abadie. Her father was a certain Pierre Abadie "stone-cutter by day at the Sabis quarry". In the spontaneity of her account Berhadette uses the family name of her best-known friend and thus more familiar to her. Jacomet took note of it by transcribing it.

4) Between the terms "**apparition**" and "**vision**" there is a certain difference. Precisely in the way in which they occur. In practice, the two words are wrongly used, without any distinction, to indicate the same phenomenon.
"**Apparition**" is prevalently an evident manifestation that affects the external senses. "**Vision**" is, by contrast, prevalently an "intellective" imaginative manifestation" which affects the inner senses. Both of them, however, as reflex and consequence, act on the visionary by creating estasy, contemplation and a certain evident transfiguration of the body.
In her deposition and autographed accounts, Bernadette usually uses the term "vision" "sometimes"apparition", but she does this without any distinction of meaning. We know, however, that hers were apparitions because they were evident manifestations of the Virgin which affected the external senses of Bernadette. Therefore, for a more precise terminology, we shall in future substitute the term "vision" by the more appropriate word "**apparition**".

5) Bernadette called the Virgin **Aquerò** until the 16th apparition when she had the certainty of the identity of the Virgin herself. The deposition drawn up by Jacomet is the first written document concerning this. Such a name is repeated more than once. For the particular meaning of such a dialect term, see "Così è nata Lourdes" by A. Bernardo, Turin: LDC Leumann, 1981, page 111.

6) Thanks to various witnesses we know that things occurred in a different way. Baloume made the stone roll to frighten her companions, out of spite. It had the desired effect. Bernadette was in an ecstasy in front of the grotto. Her frightened companions tried to escape, attempting to drag away her heavy, motionless body. They did not succeed. Because of the screams the miller Nicolau rushed up and lifted Bernadette, carrying her to the mill of Savy nearby, where she recovered consciousness.

Bernadette making her deposition before the Commission of Inquiry presided over by the bishop, Mgr. Laurence (7.12.1860).

Bernadette before the Bishop
(7-12-1860)

More than two years have elapsed since the setting up of the diocesan Commission charged with inquiring into the truth and the nature of the events of Massabielle. The subcommittee has carried out a vast amount of work by collecting hundreds of depositions with related reports.

It had examined innumerable cases of recovery, with the help of the professional expertise of medical practitioners. Now on the desk of Mgr. Laurence there was a voluminous dossier that testified to all the care employed in the task The bishop, before taking a decision about an event of such great importance and far-reaching circumstances, wished to hear Bernadette personally. Her deposition took place in the Bishop's Court of Tarbes, in the presence of the whole diocesan Commission presided over by the Bishop himself.

He would later say: "Bernadette Soubirous of Lourdes appeared before the Commission charged with the inquiry. Her deposition is in conformity with the various reports drawn up on the matter in 1858".

The handwritten text consists of eight pages. It is by Canon Forcade, Secretary of the Commission. The corrections we may note in the margin are by Fr. Peyramale, made at the end of November 1861. The following deposition is the most complete and detailed document concerning the events of Lourdes, both in relation to the oral depositions and to the autographed writings of Bernadette.

11th February 1858

"Bernadette Soubirous, a girl from Lourdes aged 12 (1) went on Thursday, 11th February 1858 to collect dry wood in the company of her sister and another friend. Going along the banks of the river they arrive in front of a grotto called Massavieille. They are separated from it by a disharge channel of the mill (Lafitte). (The mill was undergoing repairs and the channel almost dry).

Bernadette's two companions, who are barefoot, easily cross over the water and reach the grotto. Bernadette, on the other hand, is wearing shoes and asks her companions to throw some stones in the channel to enable her to cross it without having to take off her shoes. When they refuse to do so, she decides to take off her shoes.

As she is removing the first of her shoes, she is struck by a noise resembling a gust of wind agitating the nearby trees. She looks at the poplars along the banks of the river, but they are motionless. She removes her second shoe and hears another noise similar to the first. She looks towards the grotto and sees that a shrub and a rose bush situated in the aperture of an oval-shaped niche are shaking.

Inside the niche she glimpses a human figure. The figure has the appearance of a lady dressed in white with a blue girdle, a white veil over her head, a yellow rose on each of her bare feet and a rosary between her hands.

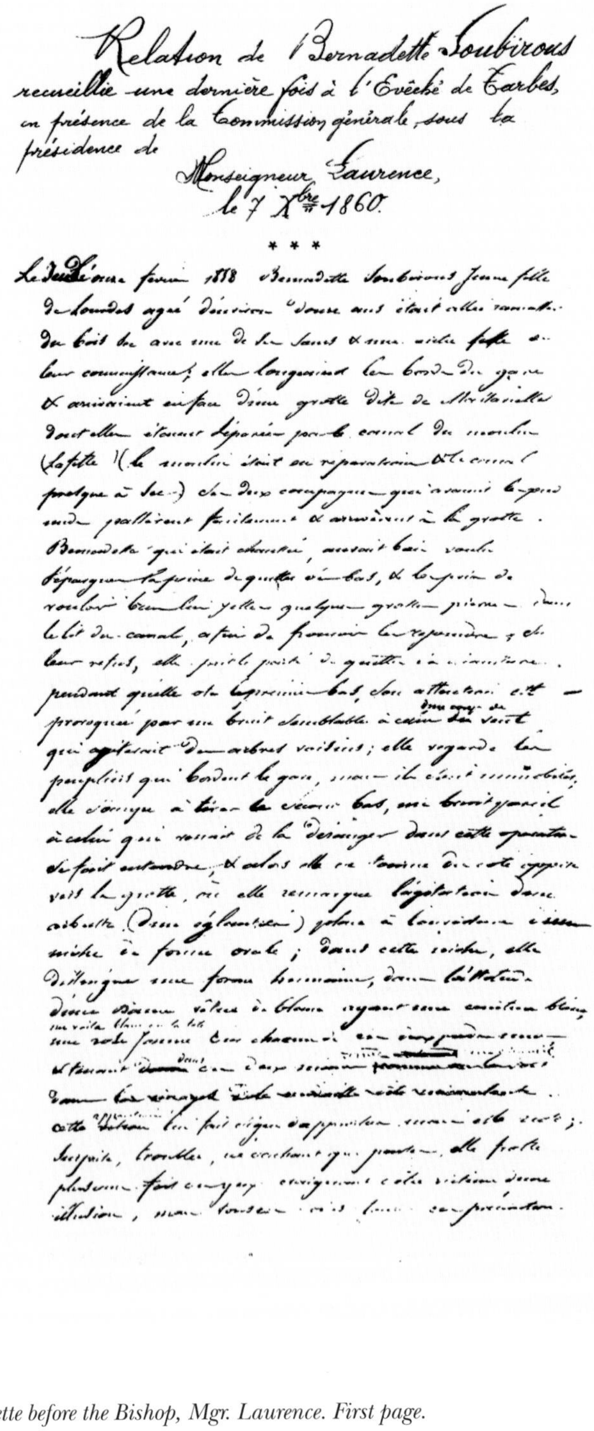

Relation de Bernadette Soubirous recueillie une dernière fois à l'Évêché de Tarbes, en présence de la Commission générale, sous la présidence de Monseigneur Laurence, le 7 X^bre 1860.

* * *

Le onze février 1858 Bernadette Soubirous jeune fille de Lourdes agée d'environ douze ans était allée ramasser du bois sec avec une de ses sœurs & une autre petite de leur connaissance; elles longeaient les bords du gave & arrivaient en face d'une grotte dite de Massabielle dont elles étaient séparées par le canal du moulin (Lafitte) (le moulin était en réparation & le canal presque à sec.) Ses deux compagnes qui avaient les pieds nus passèrent facilement & arrivèrent à la grotte. Bernadette qui était chaussée, aurait bien voulu s'épargner la peine de quitter ses bas, & les pria de vouloir bien lui jeter quelques grosses pierres dans le lit du canal, afin de pouvoir le traverser; sur leur refus, elle prit le parti de quitter ses chaussures. Pendant qu'elle ôte le premier bas, son attention est provoquée par un bruit semblable à celui d'un coup de vent qui agiterait des arbres voisins; elle regarde les peupliers qui bordent le gave, mais ils étaient immobiles; elle songe à tirer le second bas, un bruit pareil à celui qui venait de la déranger dans cette opération se fait entendre, & alors elle se tourne du côté opposé vers la grotte, où elle remarque l'agitation d'un arbuste (d'un églantier) placé à l'ouverture d'une niche en forme ovale; dans cette niche, elle distingue une forme humaine, dont l'attitude [illegible] d'une personne vêtue de blanc ayant une ceinture bleue, un voile blanc sur la tête, une robe [illegible] & tenant dans ses deux mains [illegible] [illegible]. Cette Vision lui fait signe d'approcher, mais elle n'ose; surprise, troublée, ne sachant que penser, elle frotte plusieurs fois ses yeux, craignant d'être victime d'une illusion, mais toujours [illegible]

Deposition of Bernadette before the Bishop, Mgr. Laurence. First page.

The apparition makes a gesture to her to draw near, but the girl does not dare to do so. Astonished, agitated and uncertain, she rubs her eyes several times, believing herself to be victim of an hallucination. All this serves only to confirm the reality of the apparition to her.

She is led by a pious inspiration instinctively to take out her rosary from her pocket; she tries to make the sign of the cross on her forehead, but her hand drops as if paralyzed.

She vainly tries to do so again until the apparition takes the rosary in her hand and signs herself. Encouraged by this gesture, Bernadette makes the sign of the cross and recites the rosary. At the end, the apparition disappears.

The girl finishes taking off her shoes, crosses over the channel and reaches the grotto. Her sister and friend are playing. She asks them: Didn't you see anything?

- No! - they reply, astonished by the question and probably by the emotion visible on Bernadette's face. They add:

- And you, did you see something? -

She replies evasively, trying to make them understand that she had not seen anything extraordinary. But the repeated questions of her sister and the difficulty for a girl of her age to keep a secret about such a strange event, induce Bernadette to confide something of the matter to her sister. She in turn tells her mother and Bernadette is then obliged to tell the whole story.

Louise Soubirous tries to convince her daughter that she has been the victim of an hallucination, and that her fright had made her believe something unreal. She expressly forbids her to return to the grotto".

14th February 1858

"In the meantime Antoinette, Bernadette's sister, confides the secret to various friends. Their youthful imagination is fired and they are won over by the appeal of the miraculous.

On Sunday, 14th February, they go to Bernadette to ask her to go with them to the grotto. She feels a great longing to do so, but her mother's prohibition is so solemn that she does not want in any way to disobey her. The girls do not give in and go to Louise."

"At first she refused permission. The river is so close to the grotto that an accident could occur. Not only that, but there was the risk that they would return late for Vespers and this she wanted on no account.

The GROTTO of the Apparitions. This is how it appears today to the pilgrim after the work of excavation and reconstruction carried out between 1955 and 1958 on the occasion of the Centenary of the apparitions. ▸

QUE SOY
ERA
IMMACULADA COUNCEPCIOU

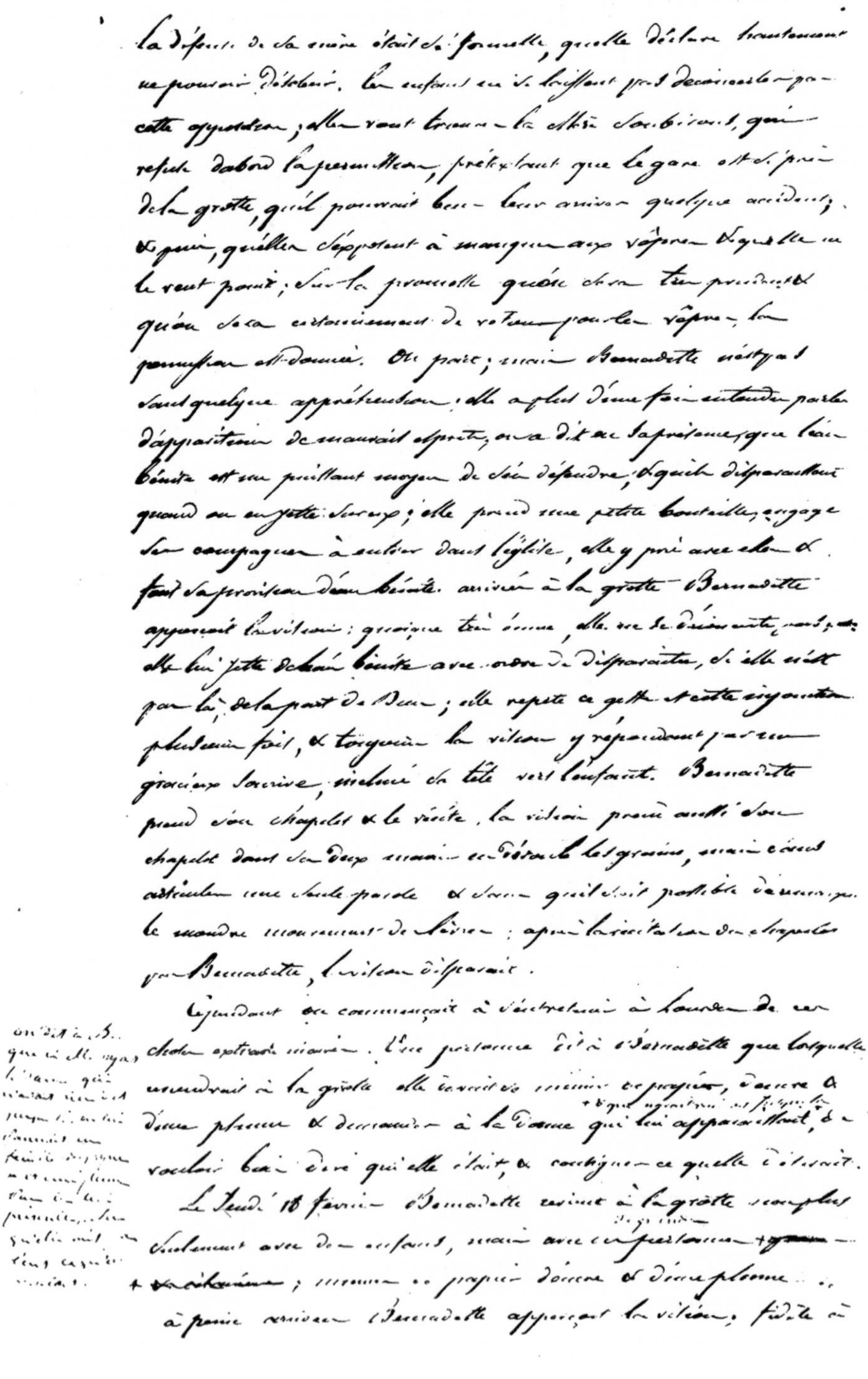

la défense de sa mère était si formelle, qu'elle déclara hautement ne pouvoir désobéir. Les enfants ne se laissant point décourager par cette opposition, allèrent trouver la Mère Soubirous, qui refusa d'abord la permission, prétextant que le gave est si près de la grotte, qu'il pourrait bien leur arriver quelque accident; et puis, qu'elles s'exposeraient à manquer aux vêpres et qu'elle ne le veut point; sur la promesse qu'on [illegible] qu'on sera exactement de retour pour les vêpres, la permission est donnée. On part; mais Bernadette n'est pas sans quelque appréhension; elle a plus d'une fois entendu parler d'apparitions de mauvais esprits, on a dit aussi en sa présence que l'eau bénite est un puissant moyen de s'en défendre, et qu'ils disparaissent quand on en jette sur eux; elle prend une petite bouteille, engage ses compagnes à entrer dans l'église, elle y prie avec elles et fait sa provision d'eau bénite. Arrivée à la grotte Bernadette aperçoit la vision; quoique très émue, elle ne se déconcerte point; mais elle lui jette de l'eau bénite avec ordre de disparaître, si elle n'est pas là de la part de Dieu; elle répète ce geste et cette injonction plusieurs fois, et toujours la vision y répondant par un gracieux sourire, incline la tête vers l'enfant. Bernadette prend son chapelet et le récite, la vision prend aussi son chapelet dans ses deux mains en défilant les grains, mais sans articuler une seule parole et sans qu'il soit possible d'apercevoir le moindre mouvement de lèvres; après la récitation du chapelet par Bernadette, la vision disparaît.

Cependant on commençait à s'entretenir à Lourdes de ces choses extraordinaires. Une personne dit à Bernadette que lorsqu'elle reviendrait à la grotte elle devrait se munir de papier, d'encre et d'une plume et demander à la Dame qui lui apparaissait, + [illegible] de vouloir bien dire qui elle était, et consigner ce qu'elle désirait.

On dit à B. que si elle n'y a[illegible] la Dame qui [illegible]

Le Jeudi 18 février Bernadette revint à la grotte non plus seulement avec des enfants, mais avec des personnes + [illegible] ; munies de papier, d'encre et d'une plume.

À peine arrivée Bernadette aperçoit la vision; fidèle à

Deposition of Bernadette before Mgr. Laurence. Third page.

But after they had promised to be careful and to return home in time for Vespers, they obtained her authorization.

They depart. But Bernadette is troubled. She feels apprehensive. She has repeatedly heard people talking about apparitions of evil spirits. They also told her that holy water is a powerful means of defence and that evil spirits vanish if sprinkled with it. She takes a little bottle and persuades her companions to go to the church. There they pray together and fill the little bottle with holy water.

On reaching the grotto, she sees the apparition. Although very excited, she tries to keep her self-control. She sprinkles the apparition with holy water and commands her to disappear if she did not come from God. She repeats the gesture and the injunction several times. The apparition replies with a gentle smile and by bowing her head. Bernadette takes out her rosary and recites it. The apparition does likewise. But she counts the beads without moving her lips or pronouncing a word. At the end,, the apparition disappears.

Meanwhile, news of these extraordinary events is spreading in Lourdes. Someone advises Bernadette to take some paper, a pen and ink with her when she returns to the grotto so as to ask the lady, who had hitherto not spoken, to put into writing who she was and what she wanted."

18th February 1858

"On Thursday 18th February Bernadette returns to the grotto in the company not only of other girls, but of some respectable persons. She is equipped with paper, pen and ink. No sooner has she arrived at the grotto than she sees the apparition. Faithful to the recommendation, she offers her the paper, pen and ink, asking her to write down her wishes. The lady smiles and replies that this wasn't necessary. She only asks the girl to have the goodness to return to the grotto for fifteen days (2). Bernadette takes out her rosary as she has done on previous occasions and recites the rosary in its entirety.

At the end of the prayer and while she is about to go away, the apparition commands her to go and drink at the fountain, to wash herself and to eat a wild herb that is to be found there. Bernadette, failing to see the water, makes her way towards the river, unable to conceive in any way how she could drink anywhere else. The apparition then calls her back and indicates the spot where she should go and drink, wash herself and eat the herb. That is, at the foot of the grotto, to the left.

She barely succeeds in reaching it, since the roof is very low.

But how is she to drink? How is she to wash herself? There were only a few drops of water, mixed with slime. She digs with her hands and forms a little hole in the ground. This slowly fills with water, but

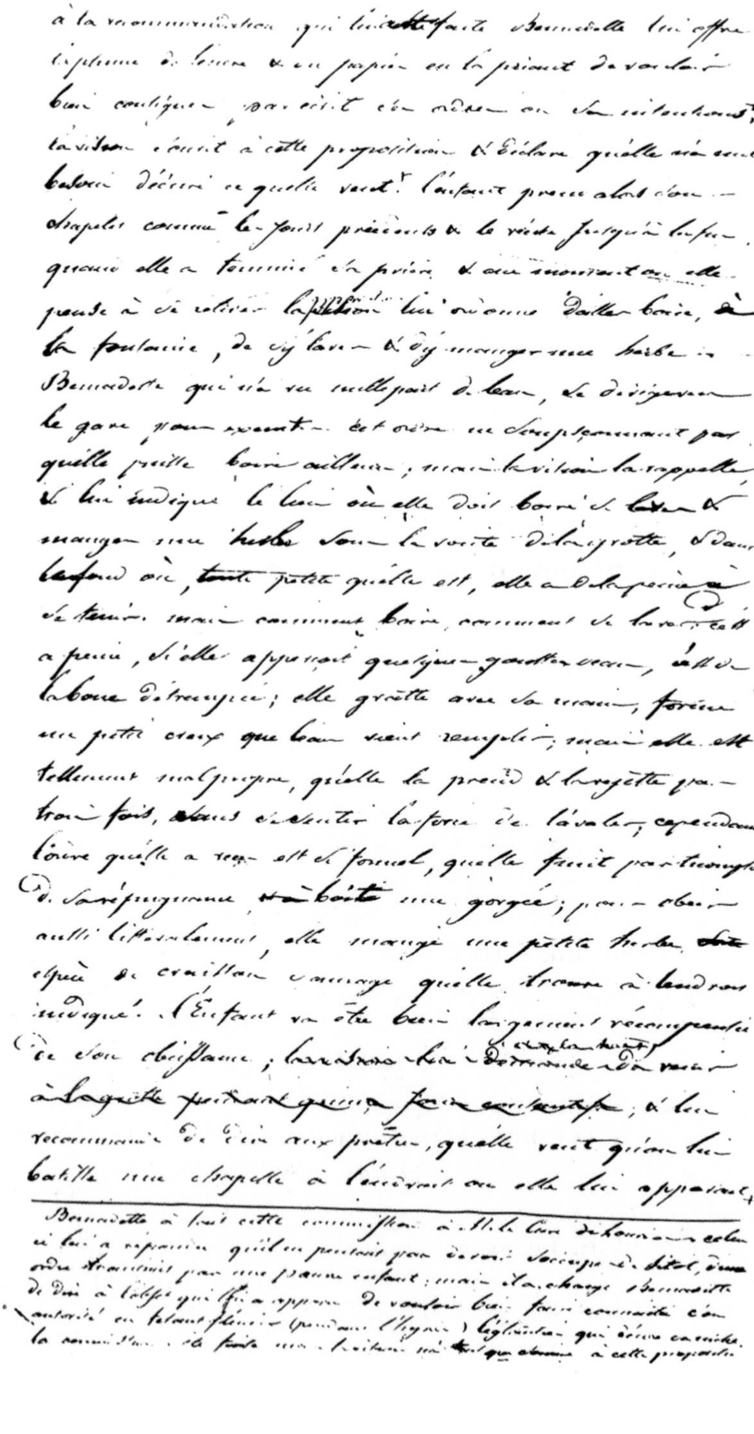

à la recommandation qui lui a été faite Bernadette lui offre
la plume de l'encre & un papier en la priant de vouloir
bien consigner par écrit ses ordres ou ses intentions;
la vision sourit à cette proposition & déclare qu'elle n'a nul
besoin d'écrire ce qu'elle veut. L'enfant prend alors son
chapelet comme les jours précédents & le récite jusqu'à la fin.
quand elle a terminé sa prière & au moment où elle
pense à se retirer l'apparition lui ordonne d'aller boire, à
la fontaine, de s'y laver & d'y manger une herbe. —
Bernadette qui n'a vu nulle part de l'eau, se dirigeait vers
le gave pour exécuter cet ordre en s'imaginant par
qu'elle pouvait boire ailleurs; mais la vision la rappelle
& lui indique le lieu où elle doit boire & laver &
manger une herbe sous la voûte de la grotte, & dans
le fond où, toute petite qu'elle est, elle a de la peine à
se tenir. mais comment boire, comment se laver? c'est
à peine, si elle aperçoit quelques gouttes d'eau, à de
la boue détrempée; elle gratte avec sa main, forme
un petit creux que l'eau vient remplir; mais elle est
tellement malpropre, qu'elle la prend & la rejette par
trois fois, sans se sentir la force de l'avaler; cependant
l'ordre qu'elle a reçu est si formel, qu'elle finit par triompher
de sa répugnance, et boit une gorgée; pour obéir
aussi littéralement, elle mange une petite herbe, sorte
espèce de cresson sauvage qu'elle trouve à l'endroit
indiqué. L'Enfant va être bien largement récompensée
de son obéissance; la vision lui demande de revenir
à laquelle pendant quinze jours consécutifs; & lui
recommande de dire aux prêtres, qu'elle veut qu'on lui
bâtisse une chapelle à l'endroit où elle lui apparaît,

Bernadette a fait cette commission à M. le Curé de Lourdes; celui-
ci lui a répondu qu'il ne pouvait pas donner suite à cet
ordre transmis par une pauvre enfant; mais il a chargé Bernadette
de dire à la Dame qui lui apparaît de vouloir bien faire connaître son
autorité en faisant fleurir (pendant l'hiver) l'églantier qui était au-dessous
la niche. [illegible] à cette proposition

Fourth page of Report. Clearly visible below is Fr. Peyramale's addition: the refusal to accept the order; the request for a proof.

it is so dirty that on three occasions on taking some of it up in her cupped hands she throws it away.

She does not have the strength to drink it. But the command she has received is so categoric that she eventually overcomes her repugnance and drinks a sip of it. And to complete the performance of the command she has received, she eats a kind of herb to be found in the place indicated. Bernadette will be copiously rewarded for this obedience.

The apparition asks Bernadette to go and tell the priests that she wishes a chapel to be built on the site of the apparitions.

(Bernadette took the commission to the parish priest of Lourdes Fr. Peyramale, who replies that he did not think it opportune to carry out a command transmitted by a poor and simple girl. He charges her to tell the apparition to reveal her identity by making the rose bush situated in the niche of the grotto burst into flower. The girl transmits the commission and in reply receives a smile". [3]

The fifteen days

"Bernadette is careful not to miss the appointment. Each day she goes to the grotto.

The news of the events spreads not only in Lourdes, but in the neighbouring parishes and in other localities of the diocese. As a consequence, when Bernadette goes to Massabielle she is followed by an increasingly numerous crowd. Sometimes she is even surrounded by several thousand onlookers.

On reaching the grotto, she begins the recitation of the rosary and those present respectfully await the moment of the apparition in meditation, in silence and in prayer. When the apparition begins, Bernadette becomes oblivious of everything. She loses a perception of everything going on around her. She becomes completely estranged from herself. Her face, irradiated by indescribable joy, clearly demonstrates that she is in contact with a supernatural being.

On two occasions during the fifteen days Bernadette did not see the apparition. More precisely, on a Monday and a Friday. She went away saddened, not knowing how to explain the reason for the absence of the favour which made her so happy. But it seems that the vision wished to compensate her for this privation by appearing to her on two further occasions after the fifteen days [4]. More precisely, on the 25th March, the feast of the Annunciation, and on the 5th April, Easter Monday".

The identity of the apparition

"On the day of the Annunciation some particular things occurred which should not be passed over in silence.

During the preceding apparitions, in response to repeated recommendations made to her, Bernadette had on several occasions asked the apparition who she was. She had only received a gentle smile in reply. This time she repeats the question with particular insistence.

The apparition, which in the past had revealed herself in the attitude of the Virgin of the Miraculous Medal (with the exception of those times when she had passed the beads of the rosary through her hands), now raises her hands, clasps them over her breast, lifts up her eyes to heaven, and in a clear voice gives the following reply: - I am the Immaculate Conception! -

Bernadette has declared that she had not previously heard anyone speaking about the Immaculate Conception and that she did not at all understand the meaning of those words which she would always treasure in her mind. Before vanishing, the apparition said to Bernadette that she promised her happiness not in this world, but in the next. She also confided to her three secrets which regarded her personally and forbade her to reveal them to anyone."

The undersigned members of the Commission guarantee the accuracy of Bernadette's deposition.

Lamole, Vicar Gen.
H. Nogaro, Dean
Lafforgue, Canon
L. Laffaille, Canon
Tabariés, Canon
Fouga, Canon
Baradère, Canon
Través, Canon
Marmouget, Canon

Tarbes, 7 décembre 1860

NOTES

(1) Error of the Commission. At the time of the apparitions Bernadette was 14 and not 12 years old. She was in fact born on 7 January 1844.

(2) The request to return to the grotto for fifteen days is a later addition in the margin by Peyramale.

(3) The same can be said about the text in italics. It is well in evidence at the foot of the reproduced manuscript.

(4) Unfounded supposition on the part of the Commission or of the drawer up of the report. Bernadette never spoke about this compensation. The two subsequent apparitions thus form part of a pre-arranged plan by the Virgin.

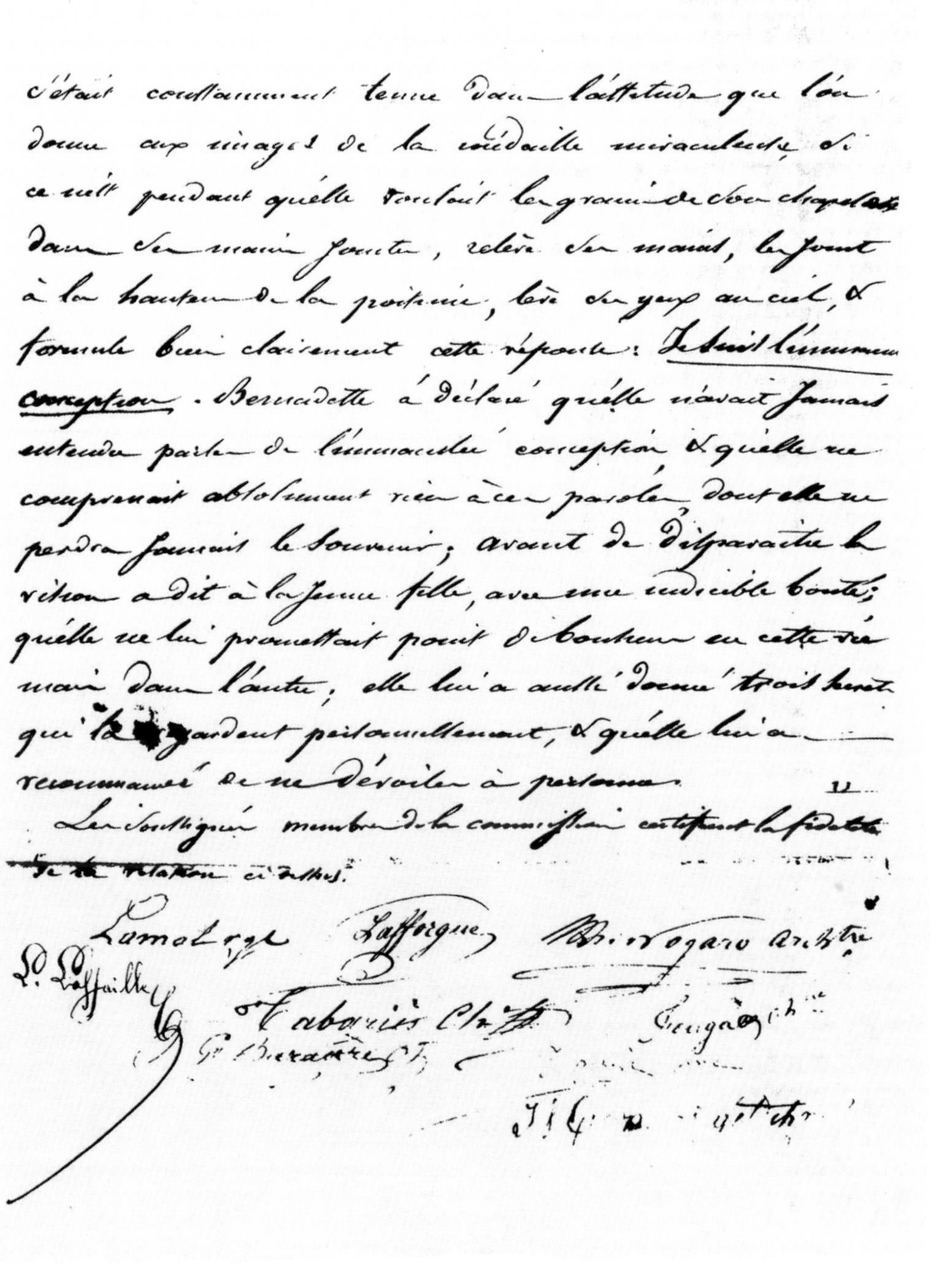
c'était constamment tenue dans l'attitude que l'on
donne aux images de la médaille miraculeuse; si
ce n'est pendant qu'elle roulait les grains de son chapelet
dans ses mains jointes, relève ses mains, les joint
à la hauteur de la poitrine, lève ses yeux au ciel, &
formule bien clairement cette réponse: Je suis l'immaculée
conception. Bernadette a déclaré qu'elle n'avait jamais
entendu parler de l'immaculée conception & qu'elle ne
comprenait absolument rien à ces paroles dont elle ne
perdra jamais le souvenir; avant de disparaître la
vision a dit à la jeune fille, avec une indicible bonté;
qu'elle ne lui promettait point le bonheur en cette vie
mais dans l'autre; elle lui a aussi donné trois secrets
qui la regardent personnellement, & qu'elle lui a
recommandé de ne dévoiler à personne.

Les soussignés membres de la commission certifient la fidélité
de la relation ci-dessus.

Lafforgue — Nogaro — Tabariès

Last Page of the report of the deposition of Bernadette signed by all the members of the Commission.

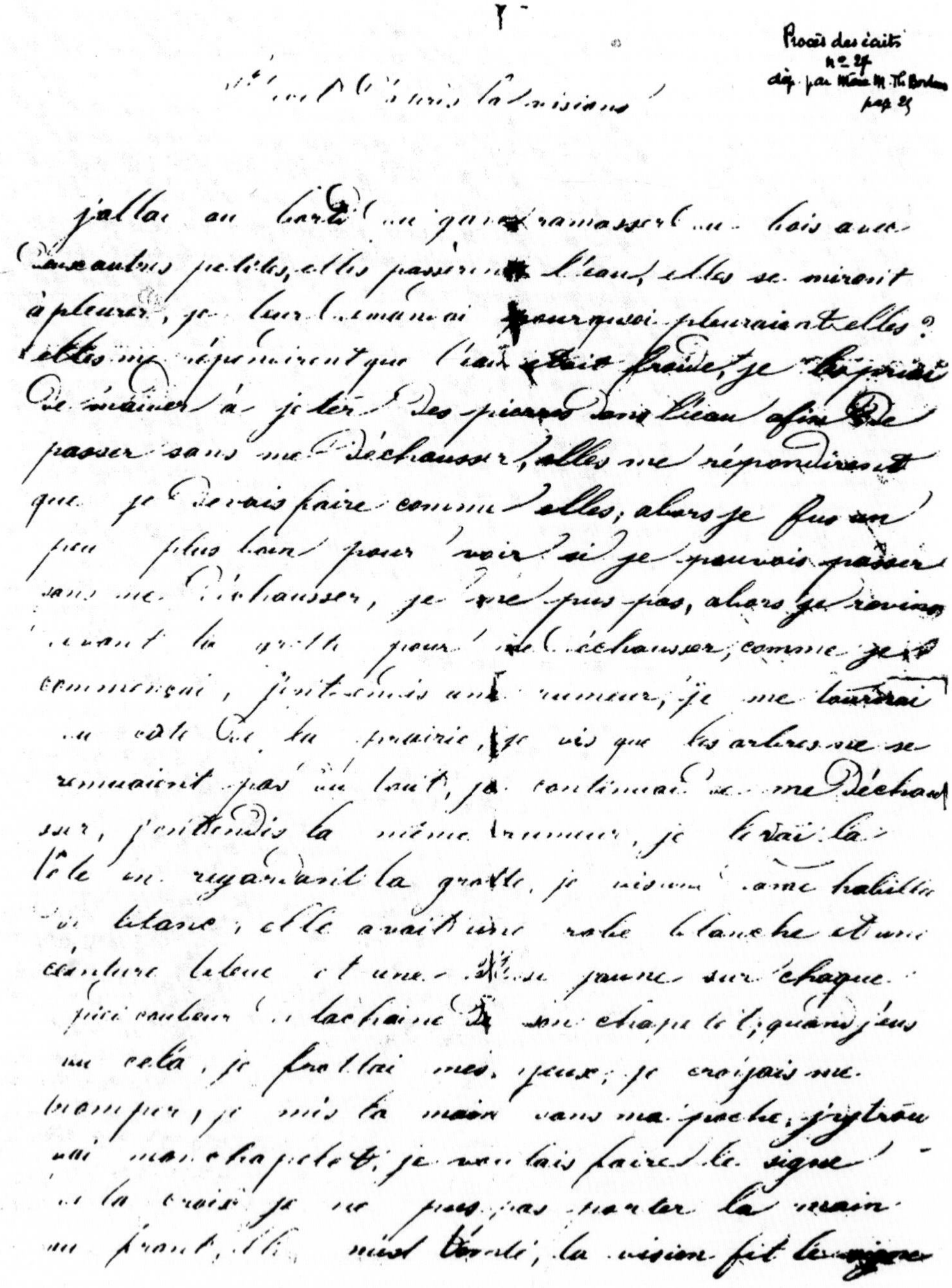

I

Procès des écrits n° 24 dép. par Mère M. Th. Bordes pag. 25

[illegible] la vision

jallai au bord de l'eau pour ramasser du bois avec deux autres petites, elles passerent l'eau, elles se mirent à pleurer, je leur demandai pourquoi pleuraient elles? elles me repondirent que l'eau etait froide, je les priai de m'aider à jeter des pierres dans l'eau afin de passer sans me déchausser, elles me répondirent que je devais faire comme elles, alors je fus un peu plus loin pour voir si je pouvais passer sans me dechausser, je ne pus pas, alors je revins devant la grotte pour me déchausser, comme je commençai, j'entendis une rumeur, je me tournai du côté de la prairie, je vis que les arbres ne se remuaient pas du tout, je continuai à me déchausser, j'entendis la même rumeur, je levai la tête en regardant la grotte, je vis une dame habillée de blanc, elle avait une robe blanche et une ceinture bleue et une rose jaune sur chaque pied couleur de la chaine de son chapelet; quand j'eus vu cela, je frottai mes yeux, je croyais me tromper, je mis la main dans ma poche, j'y trouvai mon chapelet, je voulais faire le signe de la croix je ne pus pas porter la main au front, elle me tomba, la vision fit le signe

Autographed letter of Bernadette to Father Gondrand. First page.

Letter to Father Gondrand
(28-5-1861)

"To the highly honoured Fr. Gondrand of the Oblates of Mary Immaculate - Bétharram".

This address was written by Bernadette in her own hand on a small envelope containing the letter in question.

Who was Father Ferdinand Gondrand? An Oblate of Mary Immaculate. A priest who was ordained in 1847 and was highly esteemed for his eloquence and his culture.

Towards the end of 1852 his life was abruptly shattered by some distressing family problems: he requested permission to abandon the Order and become a diocesan priest. Why did Bernadette write him this letter in which she gave an account of the apparitions? The hypotheses are various. In my view, the most probable is that, in view of the excellent relations between the Fathers of Bétharram and the sisters of the hospice of Lourdes, Fr. Gondrand had an opportunity to meet Bernadette. On such an occasion he would no doubt have asked her for an autographed account of the events at Massabielle.

In fact, at the beginning of 1861 he had gone to Lourdes to preach to the sisters at a spiritual retreat.

Why is the letter addressed to Bétharram? He often went there to visit Father Michèle Garicoits, who was in fact the founder of the Fathers of Bétharram.

But the letter never in fact reached its addressee. For when it arrived at Bétharram, Gondrand had not only left, but had abandoned the Order. And the letter was returned to Lourdes.

The letter in question is the first autographed account of the apparitions in order of time. In its concision, it forms the basis of the accounts repeated in subsequent narratives!

Report after the vision

"I went to the banks of the Gave (1) to gather firewood together with two other girls. They crossed the water and at a certain point began crying. I asked them why: they replied the water was cold.

I asked them to help me to throw some stones in the water so that I could cross over it without taking off my shoes. They replied by telling me to do as they had done if I wanted to cross. I then went a little further on in an attempt to cross, but in vain. I returned to in front of the grotto.

I had just begun to take off my shoes when I heard a noise. I turned towards the meadows but noticed that the trees were motionless. I continued taking off my shoes and once again heard the same noise.

I looked towards the grotto and saw a lady dressed in white. She had a white dress, a blue girdle and a yellow rose on each foot. The chain of her rosary was also yellow. (2)

I rubbed my eyes thinking I was the victim of an illusion. Then, I put my hand into my pocket and took out my rosary. I wanted to make the sign of the cross, but was unable to lift my hand to my

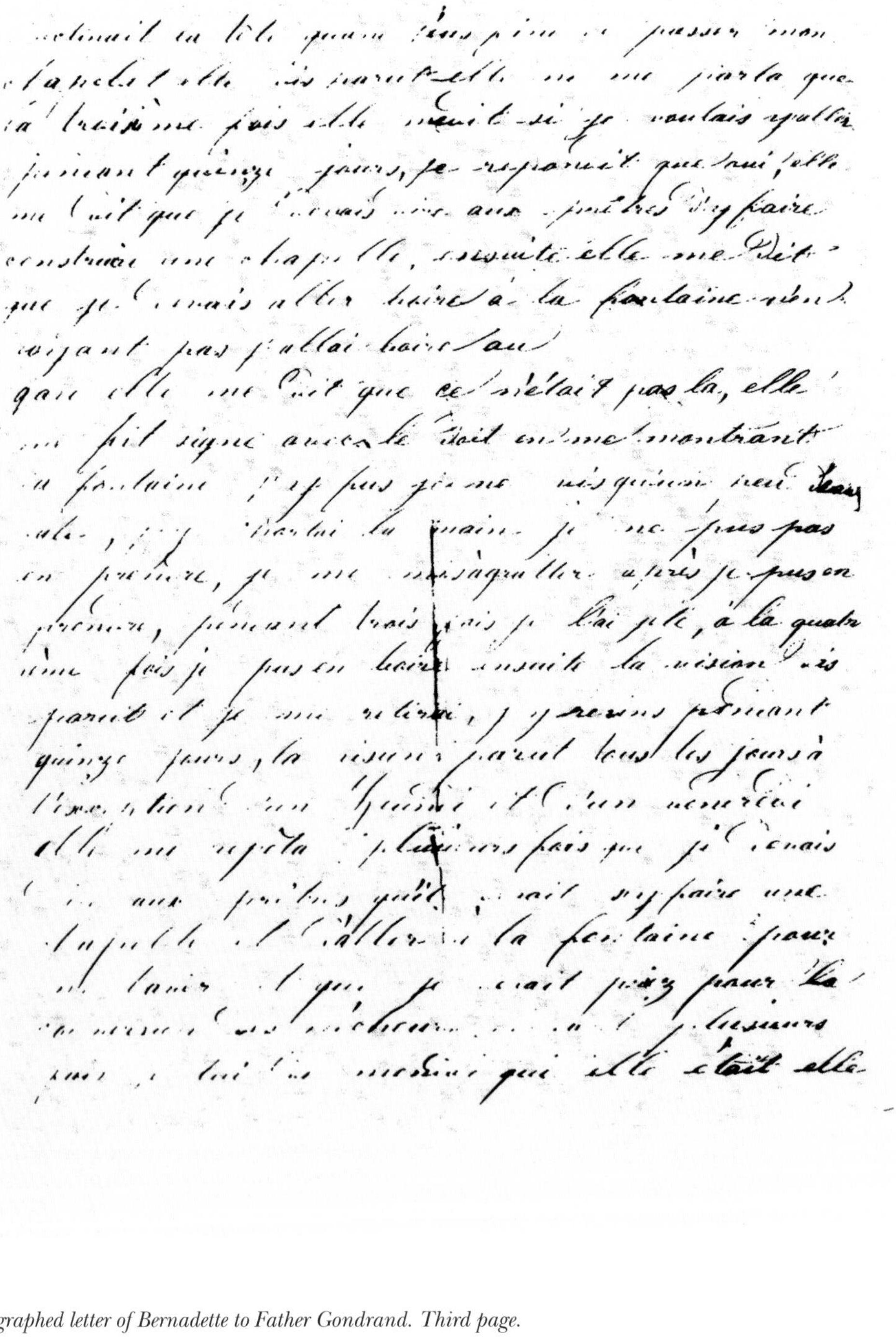

retirait sa tête quand j'eus fini de passer mon
tablier elle disparut elle ne me parla que
la troisième fois elle me dit si je voulais y aller
pendant quinze jours, je répondit que oui, elle
me dit que je devais dire aux prêtres d'y faire
construire une chapelle, ensuite elle me dit
que je devais aller boire à la fontaine n'en
voyant pas j'allai boire au gave
qand elle me dit que ce n'était pas là, elle
me fit signe avec le doit en me montrant
la fontaine j'y fus je ne vis qu'un peu d'eau
sale, j'y portai la main je ne pus pas
en prendre, je me mis à gratter après je pus en
prendre, pendant trois fois je l'ai jeté, à la quatre
ième fois je pus en boire ensuite la vision dis
parut et je me retirai, j'y revins pendant
quinze jours, la vision parut tous les jours à
l'exception d'un lundi et d'un vendredi
elle me répéta plusieurs fois que je devais
dire aux prêtres qu'il devait y faire une
chapelle et d'aller à la fontaine pour
me laver et que je devait prier pour la
conversion des pécheurs, plusieurs
fois je lui demandai qui elle était elle

Autographed letter of Bernadette to Father Gondrand. Third page.

forehead, because when I did so it fell.

The apparition made the sign of the cross: my hand was trembling. I tried to do so again and this time succeeded. I recited the rosary. The apparition threaded the beads of the rosary through her fingers without moving her lips. When she had finished, she suddenly vanished.

I asked my companions if they had seen anything. They replied that they had not. They asked me to tell them what had happened. I replied that I had seen a lady dressed in white, but did not know who she was. I asked them to say nothing about the matter; they advised me not to return to the spot any more. I said I would not.

I returned to the grotto a second time on the following Sunday because I felt an inner urge to do so.

My mother had forbidden me to do so. After Mass, two other friends and I went to her and urged that we be allowed to go. She was utterly against it. She feared I would fall into the water and return late for Vespers. I reassured her and she gave me permission.

Beforehand I went to the parish church to fill a little bottle with holy water with the aim of sprinkling the vision with it if she should appear once again at the grotto. She appeared. I then began to sprinkle her with holy water and she smiled at me and bowed her head [(3)].

On ending the rosary, she disappeared.

She spoke to me on the third apparition. She asked me whether I would like to return to the grotto for 15 days. I said yes. She added that I should tell the priests to build a chapel on the spot. Afterwards she ordered me to go and drink at the fountain.

Not seeing it, I went to drink at the river. She told me it was not there I should go to drink and indicated the fountain to me with her finger. I made my way there, but found nothing but a little muddy water. I was unable with my cupped hand to scoop it up. I then began to dig in the ground. Only in this way did I succeed, but three times I threw the water away because it was dirty. The fourth time I drank it [(4)].

The apparition disappeared and I went away. I returned to the grotto for 15 days. She always appeared to me with the exception of a Monday and a Friday.

On several occasions she repeated to me that I should go to the priests to tell them to build a chapel on the site of the apparitions. And that I should go to wash myself in the fountain and pray for the conversion of sinners.

Several times I asked her who she was, but she did nothing but smile. Lastly, keeping her arms stretched towards the ground [(5)], she raised her eyes to heaven and told me she was the Immaculate Conception.

[illegible] pu [illegible] les mains [illegible] bras [illegible] elle leva les yeux en regardant le ciel puis elle me dit qu'elle était l'Immaculée Conception. Dans l'espace des quinze jours elle me donna trois secrets qu'elle m'a défendu de dire à personne, j'ai été fidèle jusqu'à présent.

Voilà, Monsieur, le récit concernant la vision puisse vous être agréable. Je vous remercie du portrait que vous m'avez envoyé je le conserverai précieusement. Ma chère mère ~~vous est~~ très reconnaissante et vous prie d'agréer ses sentiments respectueux. Nous nous recommandons, Monsieur, à vos ferventes et saintes prières en nous unissant dans les Sacrés Coeurs de Jésus et de Marie.

Votre très humble et toute dévouée

Bernadette Soubirous

Lourdes le [illegible] Mai 1861

Last page of the autographed letter with the date and signature.

During the fifteen days she entrusted three secrets to me, forbidding me to confide them to anyone. Up to the present I have been faithful.

This is my account concerning the apparition. I hope it is agreeable to you..."

Your most humble and devoted
Bernadette Soubirous

Lourdes, 28th May 1861

NOTES

1) "**GAVE**". In the dialect of Lourdes this word meant "river". The river in question rises from the glaciers of Gavernie, traverses a large part of the French High Pyrenees, passes through the little town of Lourdes, flows in front of the grotto of Massabielle and ends by debouching into another river, the Adour near Bayonne.

2) This description differs somewhat from the deposition on 21st February 1858 before the Commissioner Jacomet:
"I heard a very loud noise coming from the hedge that was situated above the grotto. I looked in that direction and saw the hedge shaking very much. Behind it I noticed something white, like a young girl,..
The description on 21st February is more spontaneous. still under the impression of the recent apparition. In the letter of some years later. it is by contrast more thought over and elaborated.

3) In the deposition of 21st February 1858 no mention is made of the sprinkling with the holy water and of the bows and smiles of the apparition.

4) Here there is no mention of the message of Penance expressed by the Virgin. From the other narratives and from witnesses. we know that the apparition repeated the word "Penance" three times. Not only that, but she ordered Bernadette to eat a wild herb as a penance.

5) A detail which is at variance with all the other oral depositions and autographed accounts. Elsewhere Bernadette always said: she raised her hands, clasped over her breast and lifted her eyes to heaven.

The Grotto of Massabielle

"From there we followed the channel and found ourselves in front of a grotto … I raised my eyes towards the grotto and saw a lady dressed in white".

The name "Massabielle" derives from "Massavielle" which in local dialect means "old rock". The grotto of which Bernadette speaks and where the apparitions took place consists of a rock mass about 27 m. high. It was covered with bushes and ivy.

The whole rock is supported by an enormous and mighty arch which constitutes the actual grotto.

Inside, it consists of three irregular and almost communicating apertures. The largest is 8 m. deep, 5 m. wide and 6 m. high. In this rocky mass, full of protuberances and clefts, there is an oval niche on the right. It too was covered with ivy, shrubs, withered grass and especially with a bush of wild roses. The floor of the grotto was overlaid with mould mixed with sand and gravel. Here and there were dry branches, pieces of wood, animal bones thrown up by the river in flood.

All this formed an inclined floor that joined the roof of the grotto at the bottom. A water-channel flowed in front of the grotto. It was the discharge of the mill of Savy and of the adjoining sawmill. When it was in full activity the water could reach a height of 40 cm. and it ended by flowing into the nearby "Gave".

Usually the grotto was used as a natural shelter by the fishermen and hunters of the area in case of bad weather.

In the niche where the Virgin habitually appeared, a statue carved out of white Carrara marble was set up and blessed on 4 March 1864. It was carved by the sculptor Fabich of Lyons following the indications provided by Bernadette herself.

◂ *14 August 1983: Pope John Paul II, a pilgrim to Lourdes, in prayer before the Grotto of the Apparitions (Photo by A. Bernardo)*

COMMISSARIAT

The Parish Churc

"I went to the parish church to fill a little bottle with holy water with the aim of sprinkling the apparition with it if she should appear once again."

It was the parish church of St. Peter, a building in the gothic style. The apse was fortified in the XIth century to serve as a defence during the religious wars.

Here on 9th January 1843 François Soubirous and Louise Casterot celebrated their wedding. Here on 9th January 1844 Bernadette was christened.

On one of the altars stood a small Madonna of gold-painted wood preserved today at the Cachot. It represents Our Lady of the Miraculous Medal. Repeatedly Bernadette prayed before this statue.

On 25th February 1858 Bernadette appears before the Prosecutor Dutour to be interrogated. He asks her:

"Whom does your apparition resemble?"

Bernadette answers: "As regards the face and the clothes, she perfectly resembles the statue of the Virgin in the parish church. She is, however, surrounded by light and she is alive."

The old parish church no longer exists. It was demolished in 1905 because it was ruinously old and devastated by fire.

In its place a public garden was laid out, with a war memorial to the fallen of the First and Second World Wars.

The font where Bernadette was christened has been placed in the new, larger and more welcoming parish church, built a short distance away.

◂ *An exceptional historic record: original photo of the old parish church of St. Peter in Lourdes where Bernadette was baptized.*

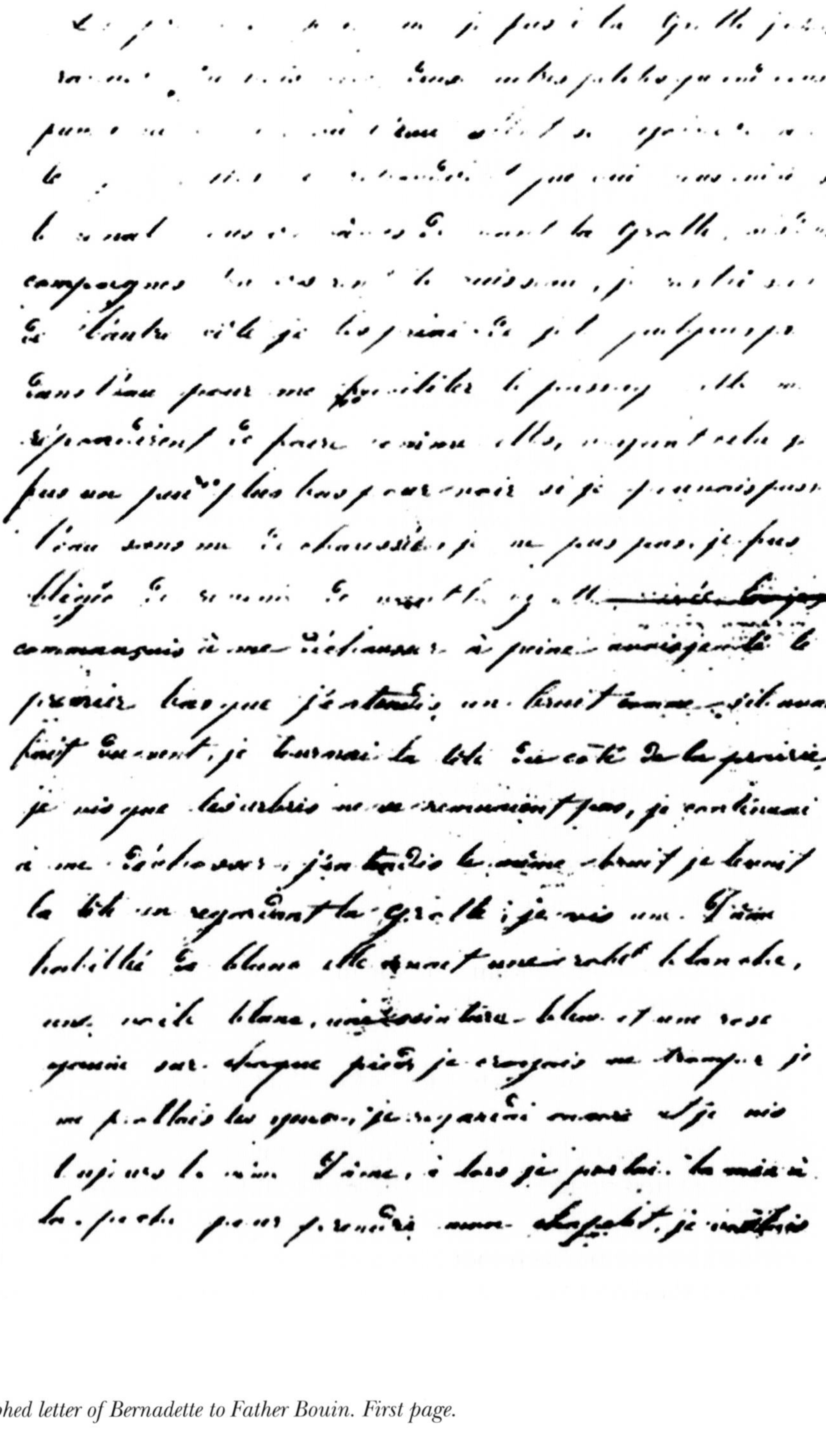

Autographed letter of Bernadette to Father Bouin. First page.

Letter to C. Bouin

(22-8-1864)

As regards the letter about the apparitions addressed by Bernadette to Charles Bouin, the following questions arise: How did Bernadette come to know this priest? How was it that Bernadette became fond of him to such a point that she sent him an account of the events of the grotto? The answer comes from Bernadette's letters of 9th July and 22nd August 1864 sent to the priest in question. Bouin came from a protestant family. He was converted and attracted to the Catholic priesthood. He was ordained on 21st December 1863. A priest of deep devotion to the Virgin Mary.

In 1864 he went on a pilgrimage to Lourdes and met Bernadette. She must have been fascinated by the spirituality of the young priest and by his devotion to the Virgin Mary. Above all she must have been moved on hearing his desire to become a hermit after the pilgrimage to Massabielle. Later on, Bouin pressed Bernadette, through a letter, to give an account of her apparitions and she satisfied his request. The dream of becoming a hermit did not come to anything, but between him and Bernadette there arose a kinship of ideals, as precisely the exchange of letters demonstrated. Bouin "had an extraordinary intelligence, a profound humility and a fascinating spirituality". Thanks to these qualities he was able to understand and appreciate the special mission of the priviliged one of Lourdes.

In its subject and structure the letter faithfully follows the one addressed to Fr. Gondrand three years previously. Two relevant annotations: in this letter Bernadette speaks of the promise of not an earthly but a heavenly bliss. And then the final phrase that closes the story: "She had blue eyes". A detail which is not met with in any other description of the apparitions.

"The first time that I was at the grotto I went to collect wood together with two other girls.

On reaching the mill, I asked them if they would like to see where the discharge water ran into the river. They said yes. We went along the channel and arrived in front of a grotto. My companions crossed the water, whereas I remained on the other side.

I asked them to throw some stones into the channel to enable me to cross over it without taking off my shoes. They told me to do as they had done if I wanted to cross.

At this point, I went a bit further down in an attempt to cross over, but didn't succeed in doing so. I returned in front of the grotto.

I began taking off my shoes. I had just taken off one shoe when I heard a noise similar to a gust of wind. I turned towards the meadows and noticed that the trees were montionless. I began taking off my other shoe and then heard the same noise.

I lifted my head towards the grotto and saw a lady dressed in white. She had a white dress, a blue girdie, a white veil over her head and a yellow rose on each foot.

I thought I had made some mistake and rubbed my eyes. I looked again and again noticed the same lady. I then put my hand in my pocket and took out my rosary.

I wanted to make the sign of the cross but was unable to do so

"The miracle of the candle" (XVIIth Apparition) by Carrier-Belleuse. (Painting from the hotel Panorama).

because I could not reach up my hand. Although filled with fear, I remained.

The apparition made the sign of the cross; I too tried to do so and succeeded. After making the sign of the cross, I calmed down and recited the rosary, with the image of the lady constantly before me.

She motioned to me with her finger to draw near, but I did not have the courage to do so and remained in the same place.

At the end of the rosary I asked my companions if they had seen anything. They replied that they had not. I pressed them again, but their reply was always in the negative. I asked them to say nothing about it to anyone. They said to me: - So you,ve seen something? -

I didn't want to tell them about it, but they urged me so much that I decided to tell them everything on condition that they would maintain absolute silence. They promised me to do so; but no sooner had they arrived home than they lost no time in saying that I had seen a lady dressed in white.

This is what happened the first time I went to the grotto. It was Thursday, 11th February 1858.

On the following Sunday I returned there a second time together with various other persons. Some people had advised me to take paper and ink with me and to ask the lady, if she should appear again, to put down in writing anything she had to say.

On reaching the spot, I began the rosary. At the end of the first ten Hail Mary's, the lady appeared and I asked her to put down in writing anything she had to say to me. She smiled and told me it was not necessary to put into writing what she had to communicate to me. She asked me to have the goodness to return to the grotto for fifteen days.

I promised her that I would do so.

She also asked me to go and tell the priests to build a chapel on the spot, to go and drink at the fountain and wash myself, and to pray for sinners. She repeated this to me several times.

She told me that she promised me happiness not in this world, but in the next.

I repeatedly asked her who she was: she only replied to me with a smile. I saw her on fifteen consecutive days, with the exception of a Monday and a Friday.

At the end of the fifteen days she told me she was the Immaculate Conception. "She had blue eyes."

Bernadette Soubirous

Lourdes, 22nd August 1864

The Spring. This is how it appears today at the foot of the Grotto to the left.

The 20 taps, to the left of the Grotto, where the pilgrim may draw water from the Spring.

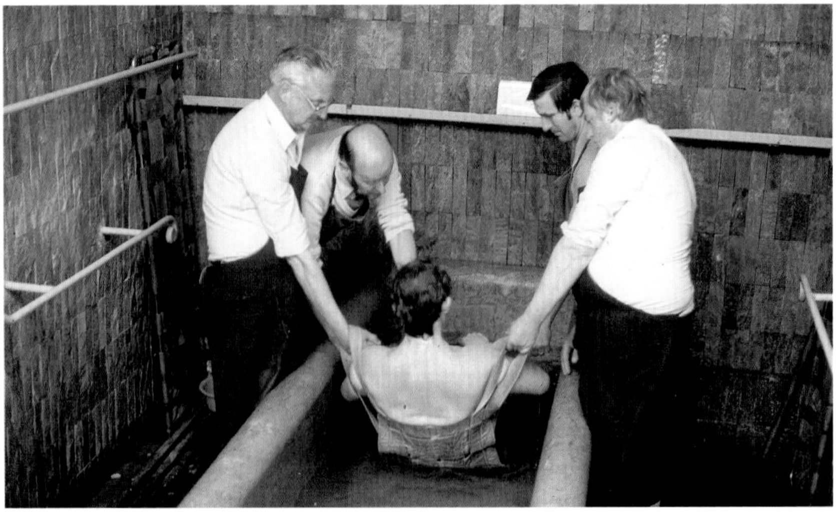

The Baths fed by the water from the Spring. Both the healthy and the sick immerse themselves in them.

The Spring

"One day she told me to go and drink at the fountain and wash myself. Since I could not see it, I went to drink at the river. She told me it wasn't there I was to go and motioned to me with her finger, indicating the fountain to me."

The behaviour of Bernadette at the foot of the grotto in obedience to the apparition gave rise to delusion and conflicting opinions; in some, it excited compassion.

They considered her crazy.

All this we know from eye-witnesses. But precisely from that moment began the destiny of the water of the grotto in Massabielle. The destiny of an invitation to purification and to the change of spiritual life. A destiny of recoveries, contradiction, analysis, devotion and deviation.

Bernadette had obeyed. She got up and went away. But the slimy water continued to gush more and more abundantly from the hole she has made. It flowed along the slope at the bottom of the grotto and gradually became clear. On the evening of 15th February 1858 the stone-cutter Louis Bouriette went and bathed his right eye, irremediably ruined by a splinter, in this water. he recovered his sight. On 28th February Biagine Soupene, suffering from chronic blepharitis, also achieved a complete recovery by washing m this water.

Again on 28th February the dying little Justine Duconte was dipped in the rudimentary basin in front of the grotto. He recovered life and health (1).

On 24th February 1858 the first rudimentary work was carried out to intercept the spring at its natural geological source, and to form a pool.

On 17th November the diocesan sub-committee of inquiry carried out an on-the-spot inspection of the grotto and the spring; Bernadette was present.

On 22nd February 1862 the floor of the grotto was cleaned of the rubble and sand to allow the water to flow in only one direction. Later, various attempts were made to reach the spring at its source.

On 11th November 1948 Mgr. Theas, bishop of Tarbes-Lourdes granted the authorization to carry out all the work necessary to reach the spring at its natural geological source and to give it a suitable systemization. The work was entrusted to the management of the well-known hydrogeological expert J. Maihlet. The work was finished in February 1949. A dual result was obtained: the reinforcement of the supply of the spring and the purification of the water from all external pollution. After this work, the spring discharges on average from 17 to 71 thousand litres of water a day, according to the period of drought or high rainfall. The spring is well in evidence at the bottom of the grotto on the left.

It has been covered with a glass sheet and illuminated.

This is how the spring at the end of the grotto is visible today on the left, after the work of systemization by the hydrogeologist J. Maihlet. It is illuminated and covered with glass.

1) See A. Bernardo. COSÌ È NATA LOURDES. Turin: LDC LEUMANN. 1981. page 154, notes 10-11-12.

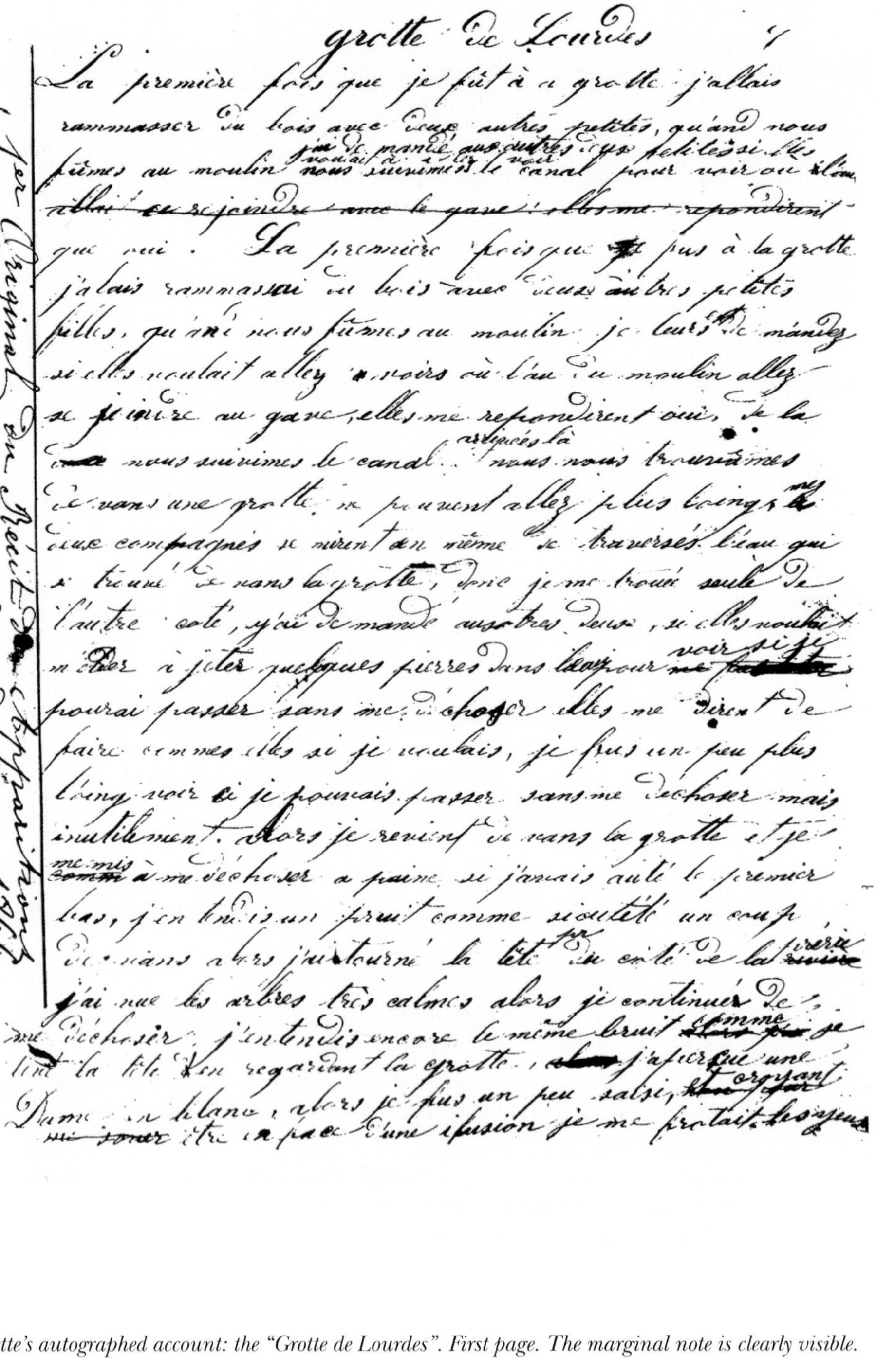
grotte de Lourdes

La première fois que je fût à a grotte j'allais rammasser du bois avec deux autres petites, quand nous fûmes au moulin nous suivimes le canal pour voir ou il allait se rejoindre avec le gave elles me repondirent que oui. La première fois que je fus à la grotte j'alais rammasser du bois avec deux autres petites filles, quand nous fûmes au moulin je leurs demandez si elles voulait allez voirs où l'au du moulin allez se joindre au gave, elles me repondirent oui, de la nous suivimes le canal. arrivées là nous nous trouvâmes devans une grotte ne pouvent allez plus loing, mes deux compagnes se mirent en mème de traversés l'eau qui se trouvé devans la grotte, donc je me trouvé seule de l'autre coté, j'ai demandé aux autres deux, si elles voulait m'aider à jeter quelques pierres dans leau pour voir si je pourai passer sans me déchoser elles me dirent de faire commes elles si je voulais, je fus un peu plus loing voir si je pouvais passer sans me déchoser mais inutilement. Alors je revins devans la grotte et je me mis à me dechoser a paine si j'avais auté le premier bas, j'en tendis un bruit comme si c'etété un coup de vans alors j'ai tourné la tête du côté de la prairie j'ai vue les arbres très calmes alors je continuai de me déchoser, j'entendis encore le même bruit comme je levé la tête en regardant la grotte, j'apercue une Dame en blanc, alors je fus un peu saisi, croyant être en face d'une ifusion je me frotait les yeux

1er Original du Récit des Apparitions écrit de la main de Bernadette en 1866

Bernadette's autographed account: the "Grotte de Lourdes". First page. The marginal note is clearly visible.

The "Grotte de Lourdes"

(Spring 1866)

The autographed account known as the "Grotte de Lourdes" deserves particular attention. It consists of three parts written in a school exercise book. It is a rough copy with many erasures and corrections. As a whole, however, it is the most detailed and complete autographed account we possess. First part: narrative of the first three apparitions with the message of the vision.

Second part: narrative of the visits of the parish priest Fr. Peyramale, and of the interrogations to which Bernadette was subjected under the Commissioner Jacomet and the Public Prosecutor Dutour.

Third part: outline of the successive draft of the "Camet" on 12th May 1866. The outline has been lost. In the third part Bernadette resumes her narrative beginning from the second apparition and concluding it with the identification of the vision. That is the only one we have.

How did the "Grotte de Lourdes" come to be?

It is the spring of 1866. Bernadette is preparing to leave for the convent of Nevers. With the help of a nun of the hospice she decides to draw up an account of the apparitions in a more organic, complete and presentable way. Perhaps she intends to copy the draft text and take it with her. The nun corrects the spelling mistakes, the punctuation and some expressions without, however, changing the substance.

Bernadette procures an exercise book with a yellow cover and begins to make a fair copy of the account. First of all she copies the spiritual elevation, then the story of the first apparition, but at the end of the third sentence she stops, writing in the middle of a line: "year 1858".

Why this interruption, this failure to resume the copying?

Perhaps she was not satisfied with the text. Perhaps she noticed some gaps or some error. The fact is that she begins the copying again, using another smaller exercise book with a stiff black cover. Perhaps she thought this second book more practical to carry with her and to preserve.

But not even the second copying was finished. Perhaps because of the sudden recurrence of illness; or perhaps because she was too busy with the preparations for departure. In this way, we are in possession today of the long rough copy entitled "Grotte de Lourdes" and of the incomplete "Carnet" drawn from it and that we will report further on.

The rough text used for the introductory spiritual elevation to the "Carnet" has been lost. In the present rough copy we can clearly notice empty pages and a gap in the story. In the left margin of the first page of the rough copy a line has been drawn. Under it we read the following sentence: "First original of the account of the apparitions, written by Bernadette in 1866".

What can we say about this marginal note? Certainly it is not by Bernadette.

QUE SOY

Is the date wrong or does it correspond to the year of the draft? It corresponds to the year of the draft of the manuscript. The line in the margin was also drawn by a different hand. The note was inserted before Bernadette began the draft of the manuscript, that is, on white paper.

Near the line there is a constant alignment of the handwriting. At the end of it, instead, the text does not keep to the previous alignment. Who drew the line and wrote the note in the margin? Most probably the nun who gave her help in producing a more detailed and correct draft of the apparitions. What meaning must be given to the expression "first original of the narrative" etc? There are two hypotheses: the first of these is that the rough copy Bernadette was going to draw up was considered by the nun as the first handwritten account of the apparitions. Therefore, she must have ignored the letters to Fr. Gondrand, those to the abbé Bouin and to the unknown lady.

A very improbable supposition.

If the note really had such a meaning Bernadette on reading in would have informed the nun. By the word "original" is meant a more organic complete and faithful description of the events in Massabielle in relation to the previous ones; considering them in this way as incomplete, free and without any chronological order. It is probably the most acceptable hypothesis, though it remains only a supposition.

Indeed, the "Grotte de Lourdes" has an organic unity and completeness that cannot be found elsewhere in Bernadette's autographed accounts.

First account

The first time I was at the grotto was when I went to gather wood together with two other girls.

On reaching the mill, I asked them if they would like to see where the water from the mill flowed into the river. They said yes.

From there we followed the channel and found ourselves before a grotto. Since we were unable to go any further, my companions began to wade across the water which ran before the grotto. I remained by myself on the other side.

I asked them to help me to throw some stones into the water to enable me to cross over without taking off my shoes, but they replied by telling me to do as they had done if I wanted to cross over. I went a bit further away in an attempt to cross without taking off my shoes, but in vain.

I returned to the front of the grotto and began to take off my shoes. I had just taken off one shoe when I heard a noise resembling a gust of wind. I turned towards the meadows and noticed that the trees were motionless. I continued taking off my shoes and once again heard the same noise.

I raised my head towards the grotto and noticed a lady dressed in white. I was astonished.

I thought I was the victim of an illusion and rubbed my eyes. In vain: I continued to see the same lady.

I then put my hand into my pocket and took out my rosary. I wanted to make the sign of the cross, but in vain because I found myself incapable of raising my hand to my forehead. I was gripped by great fear.

The lady took the rosary she had between her hands and signed herself. I too tried to do so a second time and this time succeeded. Once I had made the sign of the cross, my fear vanished.

I knelt and recited the rosary together with the beautiful lady. At the end she motioned to me to draw near, but I did not dare to do so and then she disappeared.

I removed my other shoe to cross over the channel which ran before the grotto; we then went home.

On the road back home, I asked my companions whether they had seen anything. They replied:

- No.

- And you, have you seen anything?

- Oh no! If you didn't see anything, then neither did I! - .

I didn't want to speak about it, but they urged me so much that I decided to tell them everything on condition that they kept mum. They promised to do so. But no sooner had they returned home than they were so gripped by the urge to talk that they told the whole story.

That is what happened the first time.

It was Thursday, 11th February.

I returned to the grotto a second time on the following Sunday, together with some girls. Before leaving we went to the parish church to fill a little bottle with holy water.

Once we had reached the place, each of us took out her own rosary and we knelt for the recitation of the rosary.

I had just finished the first ten Hail Mary's when I noticed the same lady. I immediately sprinkled her with the holy water, telling her to stay if she came from God; or if she didn't, to go away. I sprinkled her with ever greater insistence. The lady smiled and bowed her head. The more I sprinkled her, the more she smiled. After ending the rosary, we left.

That is what happened the second time.

I went to the grotto the third time on the following Thursday. I went together with some respectable persons who had advised me to take paper and ink with me and to ask the lady to put down in writing any communications she wished to make to me.

I reported this to the lady. She smiled and replied that it was unnecessary to put on paper what she had to say to me.

She asked me to be so kind as to return to the grotto for fifteen days. I replied that I would. She added by asking me to go to the priests and tell them to build a chapel on the spot, to go and drink at the fountain and to wash myself, and to pray for sinners.

These words she repeated to me several times.

She confided three secrets to me, forbidding me to reveal them to anyone.

She also told me that she promised me happiness not in this world, but in the next.

One day she commanded me to eat a herb which was to be found on the same spot where I had drunk."

Second account

"On the occasion of the third apparition I went to the parish priest to report to him that a lady had ordered me to go and tell the priests to build a chapel at the grotto.

He looked at me for a moment and then in a far from agreeable tone asked me:

- Who is this lady? -

I replied that I did not know. He charged me to ask her for her name and then return and report it to him.

On the following day, on arriving at the grotto and after reciting the rosary, I asked the lady on behalf of the parish priest what her name was. She did nothing but smile.

On returning home, I once again went to the parish priest to tell him that I had carried out his commission and that the lady had only replied with a smile. He told me that the lady was making fun of me and that I would do well not to return to the grotto any more. But I could not help but return.

In fact, I returned to the grotto for fifteen days and each time I asked her who she was. The reply was always a smile. After the fifteen days, I again asked three consecutive times who she was. Only on my fourth question did she tell me she was the Immaculate Conception.

I returned to the parish priest once again to report that the apparition had told me she was the Immaculate Conception. He asked me if I was quite sure about this. I replied that I was. I added that in order not to forget that name I had continually repeated it to myself all the way home.

On the first Sunday during the fifteen days, I had just come out of church when a municipal policeman took me by the hood and ordered me to follow him. I did so. Along the road, he told me that he was taking me to see the prison. I listened to him in silence. Instead, he led me before the Commissioner of Police, who asked me to take a seat in a room in which he was alone.

He offered me a chair and I sat down. He immediately took a sheet of paper and told me to tell him what had happened at the grotto. I did so.

After he had written down several lines of what I had actually told him, he added other things which were false. He then began to read out to me what he had written to check whether he had made any mistakes. I listened attentively.

After he had read several lines, I immediately realized that there were some inaccuracies in what he had written and interrupted him

energetically saying: - Monsieur, I didn't tell you that - He got angry, declaring that I had. I continually repeated that I hadn't. The argument lasted several minutes.

When he noted that I insisted in affirming that he had been mistaken and that I had not told him the matter in that way, he moved a little bit away from me and began again to read things which I had never told him about. Once again I maintained firmly that it wasn't correct.

It was always the same story. I remained there for an hour or an hour and a half. From time to time I heard thuds from behind the door and men shouting: - If you don't let her out, we'll break down the door -.

At the end, the Commissioner accompanied me to the exit. He opened the door and I noticed my father who was impatiently waiting for me together with a crowd of people who had followed me from the church.

This was the first time I was asked to appear before these gentlemen.

The second time I appeared before the imperial Prosecutor. During the same week he commissioned the same municipal policeman to notify me that I should appear before him at 6.00 p.m. I went together with my mother.

He asked me what had happened at the grotto. I told him everything and he put it into writing. Immediately afterwards, he read out to me what he had put down on paper, but in the same way as the

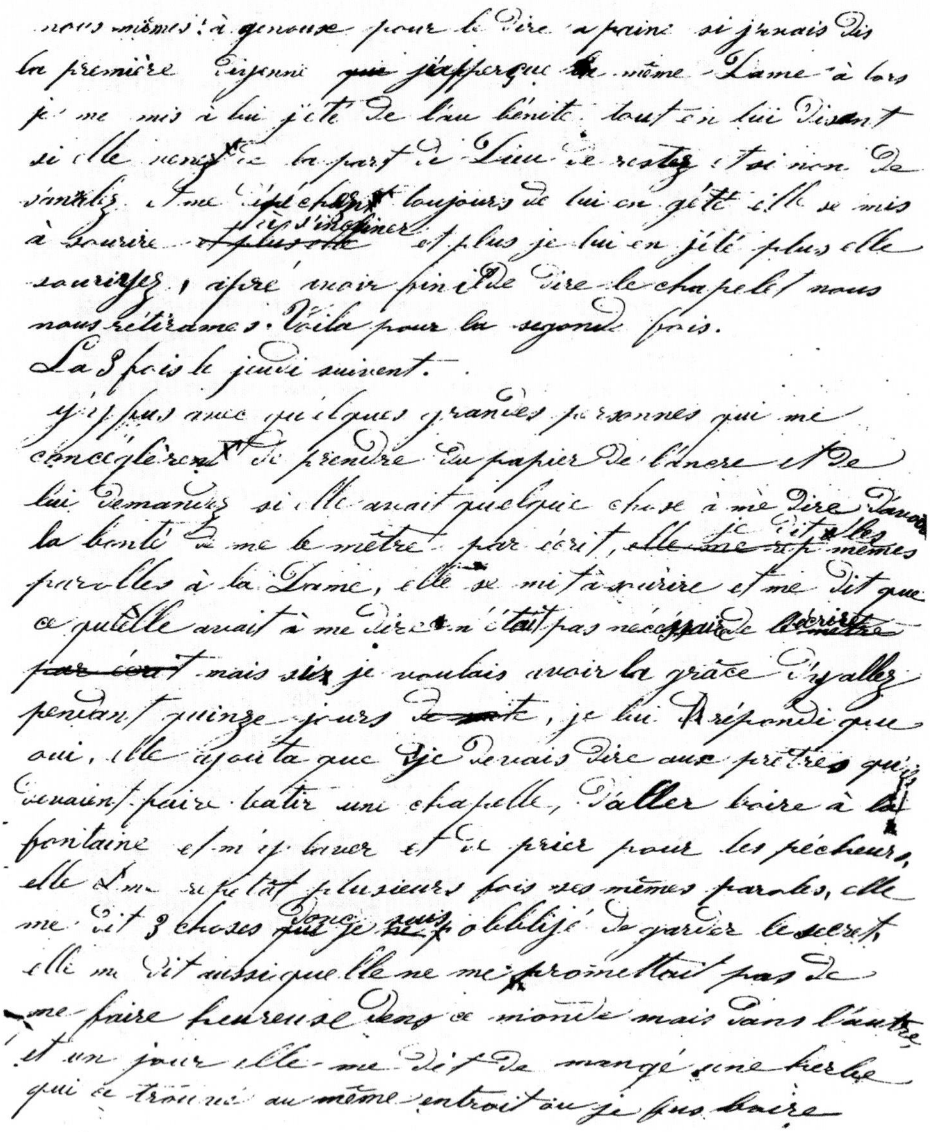

nous mêmes : à genoux pour le dire a peine si j'avais dis
la première dizenne ~~qui~~ j'apperçue la même Dame à lors
je me mis à lui jété de l'eau benite tout en lui disant
si elle venait de la part de Dieu de restez et si non de
s'en allez. Elle se mit toujours de lui en jété elle se mis
à sourire ~~et plus~~ et s'incliner et plus je lui en jété plus elle
sourissez, apres avoir fini de dire le chapelet nous
nous rétirames. Voila pour la segonde fois.
La 3 fois le jeudi suivent.
J'y fus avec quelques grandes personnes qui me
conceglèrent de prendre du papier de l'ancre et de
lui demandez si elle avait quelque chose à me dire d'avoir
la bonté de me le mètre par écrit, ~~elle me~~ je dit les mêmes
parolles à la Dame, elle se mit à sourire et me dit que
ce qu'elle avait à me dire n'était pas nécessaire de l'écrire ~~le mètre~~
~~par écrit~~ mais si je voulais avoir la grâce d'y allez
pendant quinze jours de suite, je lui répondis que
oui, elle ajouta que je devais dire aux prêtres qui
devaient faire batir une chapelle, d'aller boire à la
fontaine et m'y laver et de prier pour les pécheurs,
elle me répétat plusieurs fois ses mêmes paroles, elle
me dit 3 choses ~~qui~~ donc je ~~suis~~ s obbligé de garder le secret,
elle me dit aussi qu'elle ne me promettait pas de
me faire heureuse dans ce monde mais dans l'autre
et un jour elle me dit de mangé une herbe
qui se trouvé au même entroit où je fus boire

The "Grotte de Lourdes" - Third page.

Commissioner. That is, he had added things which I had not said.

I pointed out: - Monsieur, I didn't say that to you! - He maintained that I had. I contradicted him. After a lengthy to and fro, he told me I was wrong and continued reading. He deliberately made the same mistakes. He told me he had the Report of the Commissioner which differed from my account.

I replied that I had said the same thing to the Commissioner and that if he had made a mistake, so much the worse for him.

He then told his wife to go and call the Commissioner and a policeman to conduct me to prison. My mother began crying. From time to time she looked at me.

When she realized that they were to take me to prison, her tears increased. I consoled her by telling her: - You're right to cry for wanting to put us in prison! We haven't done anything wrong to anyone! -

While awaiting a reply, the Prosecutor, on leaving the room, offered us two chairs. My mother took one. She was all in a tremor and tired out because we had been standing on our feet for two hours. I, on the other hand, thanked him, but sat down on the floor like the stonecutters.

Outside the building some men were waiting irnpatiently. When they realized we were slow in coming out, they began banging the door, although there was a policeman there.

The Prosecutor, from time to time, leant out of the window and urged them to remain calm. They replied by telling him to let us out, otherwise they wouldn't stop. On the contrary, they would do worse.

He decided, therefore, to send us away, saying that the Commissioner had no time for the moment and that the matter would be postponed till tomorrow(1)".

Third account (2)

"The second time I returned to the, grotto was on Sunday. I went to make sure whether I hadn't made a mistake (in the company of some girls).

On reaching the spot, I knelt and began reciting the rosary. I had just finished reciting ten Hail Mary's when the same apparition appeared to me.

I had brought with me a little bottle of holy water and as soon as I saw her I sprinkled her with it. The more I sprinkled her, the more she smiled and bowed her head. In response to these gestures I took fright and hastened to sprinkle her more and more. I did so until I had completely emptied the little bottle. After I had done so, I continued reciting the rosary. The apparition disappeared before I had finished doing so. We went home to attend Vespers.

The third time was on the Thursday. I returned to the grotto in the company of a few respectable persons. On reaching the spot, I began,

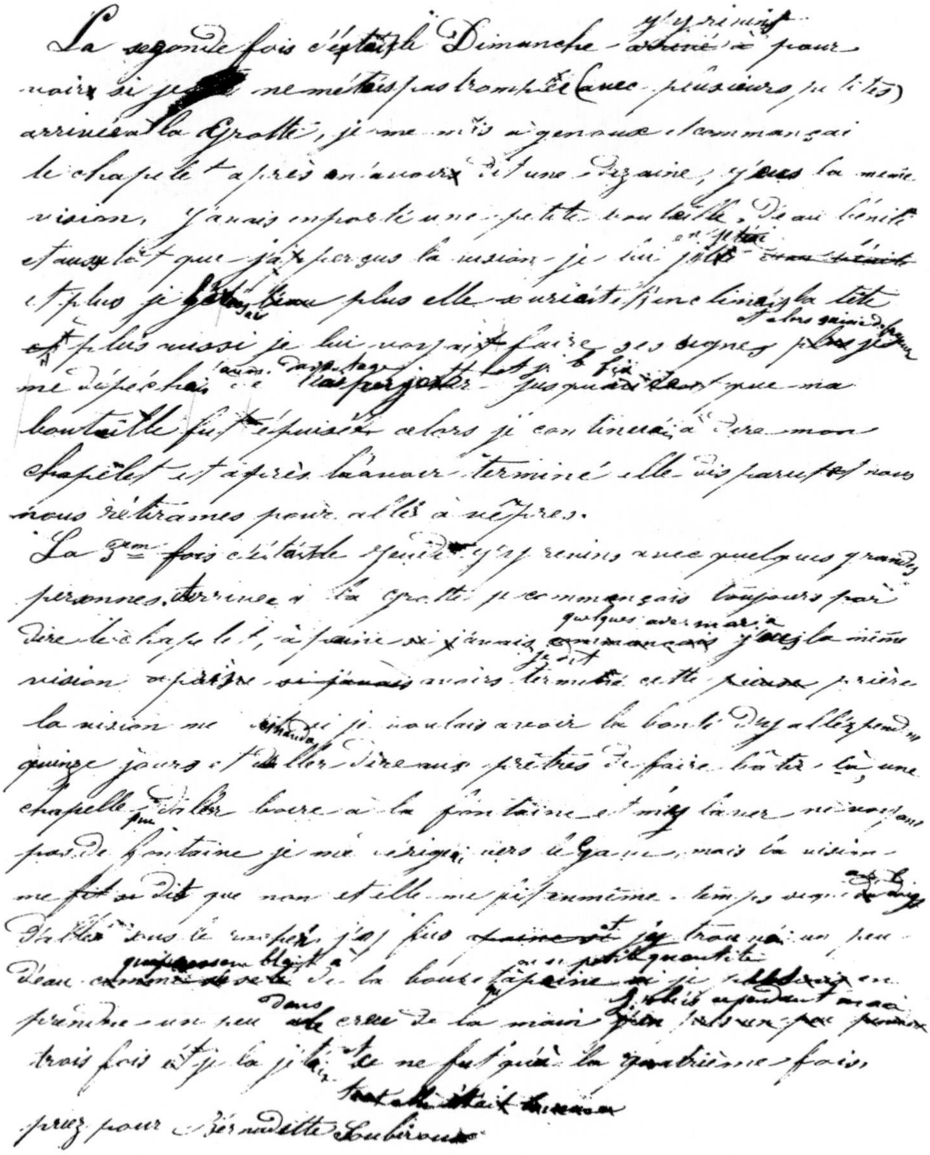
La seconde fois c'était le Dimanche j'y revins pour voir si je ne m'étais pas trompée (avec plusieurs petites) arrivée à la Grotte, je me mis à genoux et commençai le chapelet après en avoir dit une dizaine, j'eus la même vision, j'avais emporté une petite bouteille d'eau bénite et aussitôt que j'eus perçu la vision je lui en jetai et plus je lui en jetai plus elle souriait et inclinait la tête et plus aussi je lui voyais faire des signes alors saisie de peur je me dépêchai de lui asperger jusqu'à ce que ma bouteille fut épuisée alors je continuai à dire mon chapelet et après l'avoir terminé elle disparut et nous nous retirâmes pour aller à vêpres.

La 3me fois c'était le Jeudi j'y revins avec quelques grandes personnes. arrivée à la Grotte je commençai toujours par dire le chapelet, à peine j'avais dit quelques ave maria j'eus la même vision après avoir terminé cette prière la vision me dit si je voulais avoir la bonté d'y aller pendant quinze jours et d'aller dire aux prêtres de faire bâtir là une chapelle puis d'aller boire à la fontaine et m'y laver ne voyant pas de fontaine je me dirigeai vers le Gave, mais la vision me dit que non et elle me fit en même temps signe du doigt d'aller sous le rocher, j'y fus et je trouvai un peu d'eau qui paraissait bourbeuse à peine si je pus en prendre un peu dans le creux de la main je l'ai cependant ... trois fois et je la jetai. Ce ne fut qu'à la quatrième fois.

priez pour Bernadette Soubirous

The "Grotte de Lourdes". Last page.

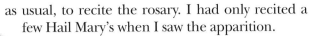

as usual, to recite the rosary. I had only recited a few Hail Mary's when I saw the apparition.

She asked me to have the goodness to return to the grotto for fifteen days. She told me to go and tell the priests to build a chapel on the site, to go and drink at the fountain and to wash myself.

Not seeing the fountain, I made my way towards the river. She told me it wasn't there and indicated to me with her finger to go to the bottom of the grotto. I went there and found only a little slimy water. There was so little of it I had difficulty in scooping it up in my cupped hands.

I tried to obey her instruction, but three times I threw the water away. It was so dirty that it was only on the fourth time that I couid bring myself to drink it.

This merciful queen also told me to pray for the conversion of sinners. She repeated these words to me several times.

During the fifteen days I asked her who she was. To the question she merely replied with a smile.

After the fifteen days were over, I once again asked her who she was three consecutive times. She continued to smile. I did so a fourth time. It was only then that she clasped her hands over her breast and told me she was the Immaculate Conception. These were the last words she addressed to me. Previously, this tender mother had confided three secrets to me which I cannot reveal to anyone".

At this point the reader may notice an interesting detail in the manuscript, to the side: a rough copy of a school dictation. At the foot of the page, moreover, some spontaneous and disconnected expressions may be seen. It should not be forgotten that Bernadette used a school exercise book for her narrative.

NOTES

(1) This second part is unique and differs from all the other manuscript accounts. It is only here that Bernadette speaks of the repeated commissions to the parish priest and the two interrogations by Jacomet and Dutour.

(2) The text of this third part was copied out again word for word by Bernadette in the "Carnet.". As a whole it is a repetition of the first. Therefore written subsequently. Why this repetition? Having finished the spiritual elevation (which has been lost), Bernadette began her account of the apparitions anew since she wanted to produce a better text than the previous one.

The Parish Priest Father Peyramale

"I went to the parish priest to report to him that the lady had ordered me to tell the priests to build a chapel at the grotto. He looked at me for a moment and then in a far from reassuring tone asked me: -Who is this lady? I told him I didn't know -".

***Domenique Marie Peyramale** was born on 9th January 1811. He officially took possession of the parish church of St. Peter in Lourdes about the second half of December 1854, a few days after the proclamation of the dogma of the Immaculate Conception. He was parish priest of Lourdes from 1854 to 1872.*

Together with the Commissioner Jacomet, he was the character most involved in the events of Massabielle. A tall, robust man, with a polite, rude or business-like manner according to circumstance. He inspired Bernadette with great fear and respect. With regard to the apparitions he maintained an initially distrustful attitude, dictated by his habitual prudence. Submissive to the instructions of the Bishop he forbade his assistant priests and the nun to go to the grotto. He followed the events at a distance. He was well informed about all that happened behind the scenes.

Bernadette went to him four times; three times to convey to him the wish of the apparition, but he did not believe in her words at all. He behaved rudely to her.

*He demanded at least that **Aquerò** should say who she was. On 25th March 1858 Bernadette told him with light and joy in her eyes the identity of the Lady, even though she did not understand the meaning of it. But Peyramale understood. Once sure of the real nature of the apparition, he became the supporter of Bernadette and of the events at the grotto.*

The construction of the crypt and of the Basilica of Our Lady in Lourdes is attributed to him. Bernadette left for the convent of Nevers. Fr. Peymarale would always be near her even though physically so far away. He constantly wrote to her.

His letters are full of paternal encouragement in her suffering, and wise advice. And she listened to the parish priest who once inspired her with such great respect and fear.

Fr. Peyramale died on 7th September 1877. It was a real father that Bernadette mourned when she learnt the news of his death. His body rests in the crypt of the new parish church of Lourdes.

The Public Prosecutor Dutour

"On the second occasion, I appeared before the imperial Prosecutor. I went to him together with my mother. He asked me what had happened at the grotto. I told him everything."

Jacques Vital Dutour *was born on 10th November 1816 in Cazeaux Villecomtal, Departement of Gers at the borders of the High Pyrenees. He was Public Prosecutor of Lourdes from 21st January 1852 to 31st March 1860 and therefore during the apparitions and the period of the diocesan inquiry on the events of Lourdes. From 1850 to 1852 he was Assistant Public Prosecutor in Tarbes, Departement of the High Pyrenees. In this function he showed zeal and great level-headedness. Undoubtedly his appointment as Public Prosecutor in the little town of Lourdes was a promotion. His attitude towards Bernadette and the events of Lourdes was greatly influenced and conditioned by the Commissioner Jacomet.*

Like him he maintained a distrustful and threatening attitude. The two interrogations of Bernadette on 21 th February and 18th March 1858 are proof of this. Like Jacomet, he had a deep-rooted conviction that the daughter of the poor miller François Soubirous suffered from hallucinations or was paid and made an instrument of those who had an interest in substantiating the story of the grotto. Like Jacomet, he was the supporter of a hard line, in favour of drastic measures as regards the "case of Massabielle" in order to put an end to the continuous and ever increasing influx of crowds to the grotto.

Twenty years after these events, encouraged and supported by the various letters of Father Cros, he wrote a monograph of 60 pages, concerning the apparitions. It is, however, no more than a collection of fragmentary notes and remarks drawn from his "Reports" and therefore of little importance from the historical and factual point of view. Instead, his "Reports" on the events of Lourdes, sent to the Attorney General of Pau, have greater importance.

Dutour's most valuable document, the notes on the interrogation of Bernadette on 21th February 1858, have disappeared. They were undoubtedly destroyed by Dutour himself in 1878 during the rearrangment of his personal archives.

Twenty year later, the events of Lourdes had changed him a lot. Both the notes of the interrogation and other notes must have weighed on him as a worrying accusation of his past behaviour.

He died in Pau, Departement of the Atlantic Pyrenees, in 1887.

Le 11 Mai 1866

Que mon âme était heureuse,
bonne Mère, quand j'avais
le bonheur de vous contempler
que j'aime à me rappeler ces doux
moments passés sous vos yeux
pleins de bonté et de miséricorde
pour nous. Oui bonne Mère
vous vous êtes abaissée jusqu'à terre
pour apparaître à une faible
enfant et lui communiquer certaines
choses malgré sa grande indignité
mais c'est l'humilité et la
bonté, la Reine du ciel et de
la terre a bien voulu se servir
de ce qu'il y a de plus faible

Bernadette's "Carnet"

(2-5-1866)

In her first attempt to make a fair copy of this "Carnet", Bernadette had given it a singular title: "Perhaps it expressed better what Bernadette wished to say through this account. It was to be a supreme act of gratitude to the Virgin, who had appeared to her at the grotto. A month and half later she would leave for Nevers, taking the fair copy of the "Carnet" with her, and leaving in Lourdes the Diary with the original title".

The "Carnet" is dated simply 12th May 1866. It opens with a sort of spiritual and pious effusion. In it we perceive in some way the inner feeling of Bernadette: happiness, gratitude, humility in the recollection of the apparitions, the wish for a religious life, etc.

12th May 1866

"How happy my soul was, beloved Mother,
when I so fortunately could contemplate you!
What joy in recalling the sweet moments spent under your gaze,
you who are all goodness and compassion for us!
Oh yes! affectionate Mother, you lowered yourself to the ground
to appear to a weak girl and communicate messages to her!
This, in spite of her unworthiness.
What a gesture of humility is yours!
Queen of heaven and of earth,
you made use of the weakest that existed,
in the eyes of the world!
O Mary, give the precious virtue of humility to her
who dares call herself your daughter!
Affectionate Mother, may I imitate you in everything
and for everything!
May I be a daughter according to your heart;
according to the heart of Your Son! You know it:
what great good fortune it would be for me to consecrate myself
to the religious life with the aim of serving you
and your Son better!
I put my every intention under your protection.
I pray to you: remove every obstacle that should ever present itself!
You can do so better than anyone!"

"Apparition of the Blessed Virgin at the grotto. The first time I went to the grotto was on Thursday, 11th February 1858. I went there to collect wood together with two other girls.

We made our way towards the grotto. On arriving opposite it, we

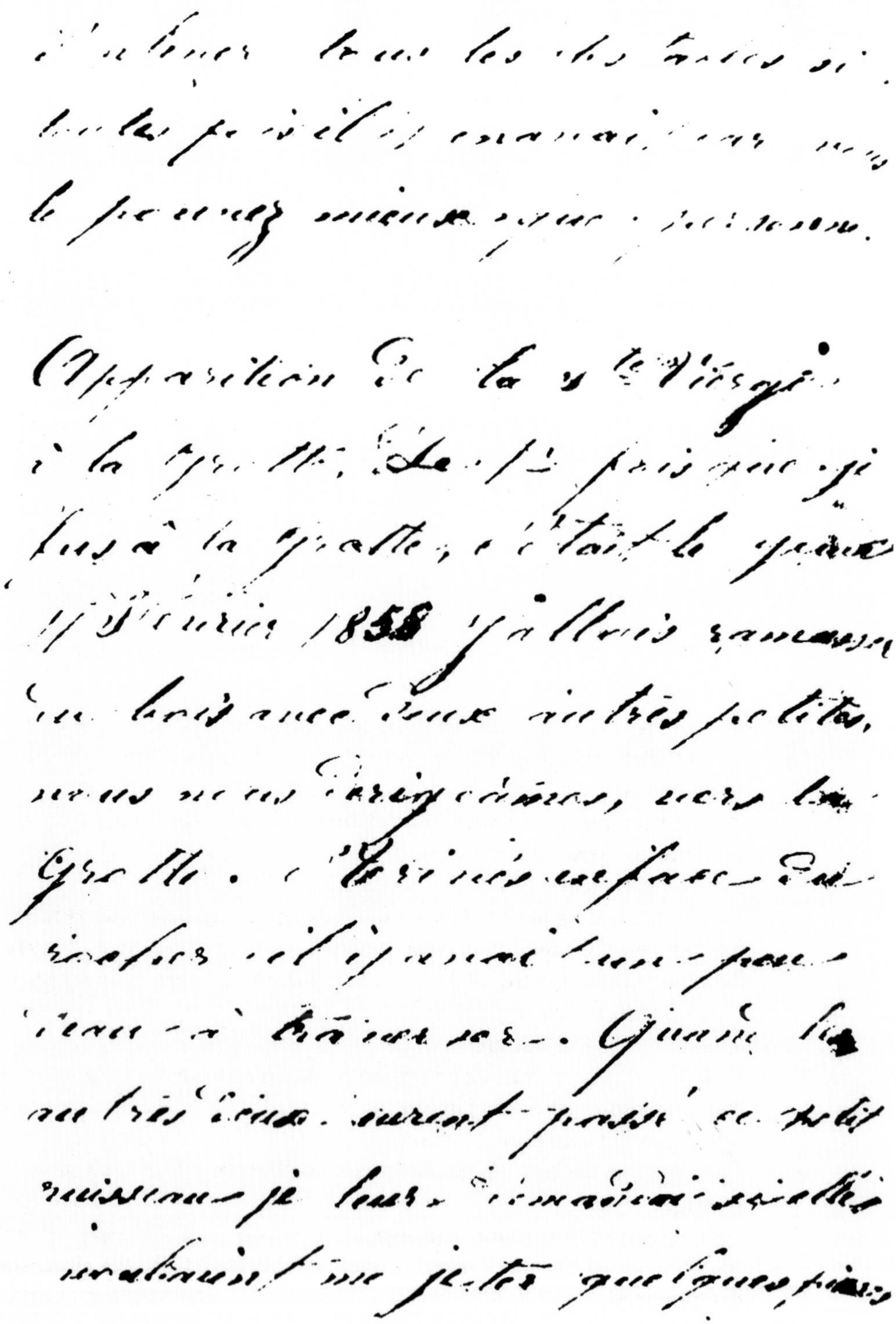

Third page of the "Carnet". It is clearly visible where Bernadette ended the spiritual elevation and began the narrative account of the apparitions.

Last page of the "Carnet" interrupted in Bernadette's copying at the word "Gave".

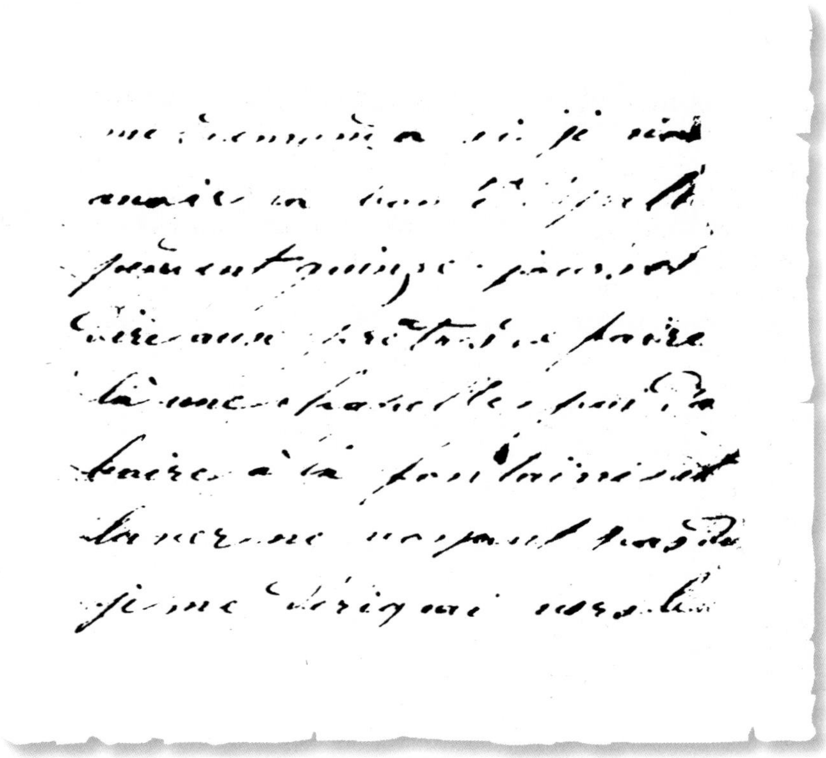

needed to cross a small stream. My companions crossed over the stream and I asked them whether they would throw some stones into the water so that I could cross without taking off my shoes.

But they refused. I went a little further on. Seeing that it was impossible to cross over without taking off my shoes, I returned to in front of the grotto.

I began taking off my shoes. I had just begun to do so when I heard a noise resembling a gust of wind. I turned my head in the opposite direction to the grotto and noticed that the trees were motionless.

I continued taking off my shoes. I once again heard the same noise. I looked at the grotto and saw the Blessed Virgin.

I thought I was the victim of an hallucination. I rubbed my eyes, but kept seeing the same image. I was filled with fear. I put my hand in my pocket and found my rosary. I took it out. I tried to make the sign of the cross but was unable to do so. Then my fear became even stronger.

The apparition made the sign of the cross with the rosary. I too tried to do so and succeeded. I recited the rosary. At the end, she disappeared.

Before beginning to recite the rosary, she had motioned to me to draw near, but I did not dare to do so.

The second time I went to the grotto was on Sunday. I returned there in the company of a few girls because I wanted to make sure whether I hadn't made a mistake.

On arriving at the grotto, I knelt and began to recite the rosary. I had just recited ten Hail Mary's when I saw the same apparition.

I had brought with me a little bottle of holy water. As soon as I saw her, I sprinkled her with it. But the more I sprinkled her with it, the more she smiled and bowed her head. These gestures frightened me and I sprinkled her more and more. I did so until I had completely emptied the little bottle. After which I continued to recite the rosary. Before ending it, the apparition had disappeared. We returned home for Vespers.

The third time was on Thursday. I returned to the grotto in the company of some respectable persons. Once on the spot, as usual, I began reciting the rosary and, after a few Hail Mary's, saw the apparition.

On ending my prayer, she asked me to have the goodness to return to the grotto for fifteen days. She told me to go and tell the priests to build a chapel on the spot; and to go and drink at the fountain, and wash myself. Not seeing it, I made my way towards the river..."

The Grotto at the time of the Apparitions. (Museum of "Petit Lourdes").

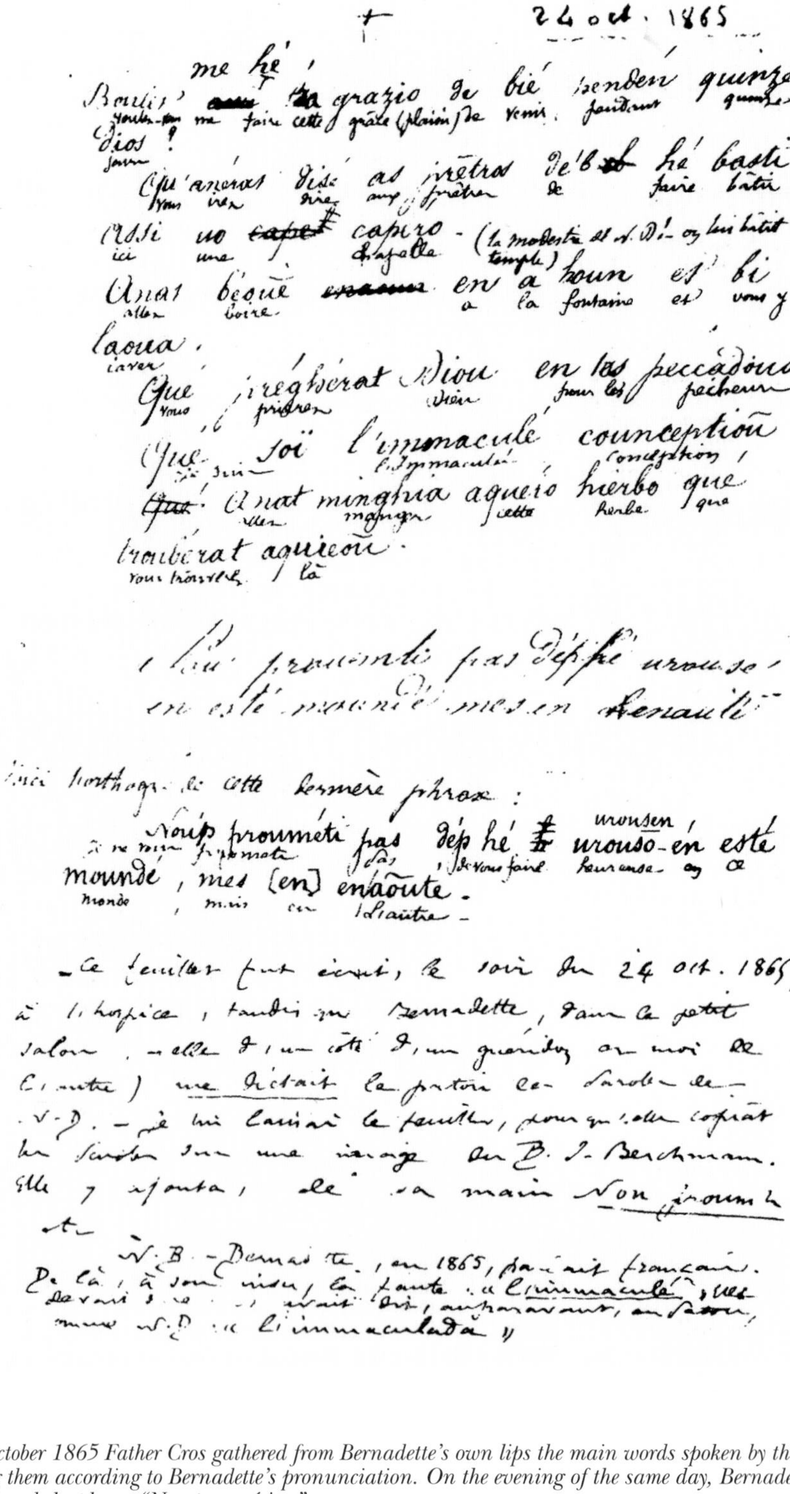
+ 24 oct. 1865

me hé
Boulès la grazio de bie' bendeu quinze dios ?
voulez-vous me faire cette grâce (plaisir) de venir, pendant quinze jours

Que' anerat dise' as prétras de'b hé basti assi uo capero - (la modestie de N.-D. - ou lui bâtit un temple)
vous irez dire aux prêtres de faire bâtir ici une chapelle

Anat béoué en a houn es bi laoua.
aller boire à la fontaine et vous y laver

Que pregarérat Diou en las peccadous
vous prierez Dieu pour les pécheurs -

Que soï l'immaculé councepciou
Je suis l'Immaculée Conception

Anat minghia aquéro hierbo que troubérat aquiéou
aller manger cette herbe que vous trouverez là

Nou prouméti pas dép hé urouso en esté mounde mes en aouté

(ici l'orthogr. de cette dernière phrase :
Nou'p prouméti pas dép hé urouso-en esté mounde, mes (en) enaoute.
Je ne vous promets pas de vous faire heureuse en ce monde, mais en l'autre -

– Ce feuillet fut écrit, le soir du 24 oct. 1865, à l'hospice, tandis que Bernadette, dans le petit salon, (elle d'un côté, moi de l'autre) me dictait les paroles de N.-D. – je lui laissai le feuillet, pour qu'elle copiât les paroles sur une image du B. J. Berchmans. Elle y ajouta, de sa main Nou proumèto.

N.B. – Bernadette, en 1865, parlait français. De là, à son insu, la faute « l'immaculée », elle avait dit, auparavant, en patois, « l'immaculada »

On 24 October 1865 Father Cros gathered from Bernadette's own lips the main words spoken by the Virgin, correcting them according to Bernadette's pronunciation. On the evening of the same day, Bernadette added in her own hand the phrase "Nou prouméti…".

Transcribed words
(24-10-1865)

On 24th October 1865 Fr. Cros, a parish priest, was passing though Lourdes. He asked Bernadette to dictate to him in the Bigourdan dialect the main words she had heard from the Virgin during the apparitions. Bernadette satisfied his wish.

She dictated and he wrote. He corrected many times the spelling and the accents according to Bernadette's indications until she was satisfied. Then he begged her to copy the Virgin's words exactly at the back of a picture of St John Berchmans. We have, therefore, the two texts herewith reported. What can we say about the original text and the transcription?

First of all, the words do not follow the chronological order of the facts. It may be supposed that Bernadette, unworried about the correctness of the words, did not take their chronology into account in dictating them.

The text is incomplete. The words of the Virgin are missing: "That isn't necessary!" (18 February 1858), "Penance! Penance! Penance! (24 February 1858), and "Kiss the ground as a sign of penance for sinners" (24 February 1858).

How to explain such an omission? For reasons of space? (size of the holy picture: 6x10.3 cm.). Certainly not! In the rough copy they are missing just the same, and there is still space. It is more probably an oversight or a free choice on the part of Bernadette. Cros relates as regards this a detail that would confirm the second supposition.

He says that in the evening Bernadette remembered having forgotten the phrase: "I do not promise you happiness in this world. but in the next" and she added it first in the rough copy, then at the bottom of the holy picture. Finally, two particulars: Bernadette uses the French word "Immaculée" instead of the Bigourdan word "Immaculade".

At the side, the holy picture bears not only the autograph of Bernadette, but also the transcription: "8 bre, lè 24, 1865".

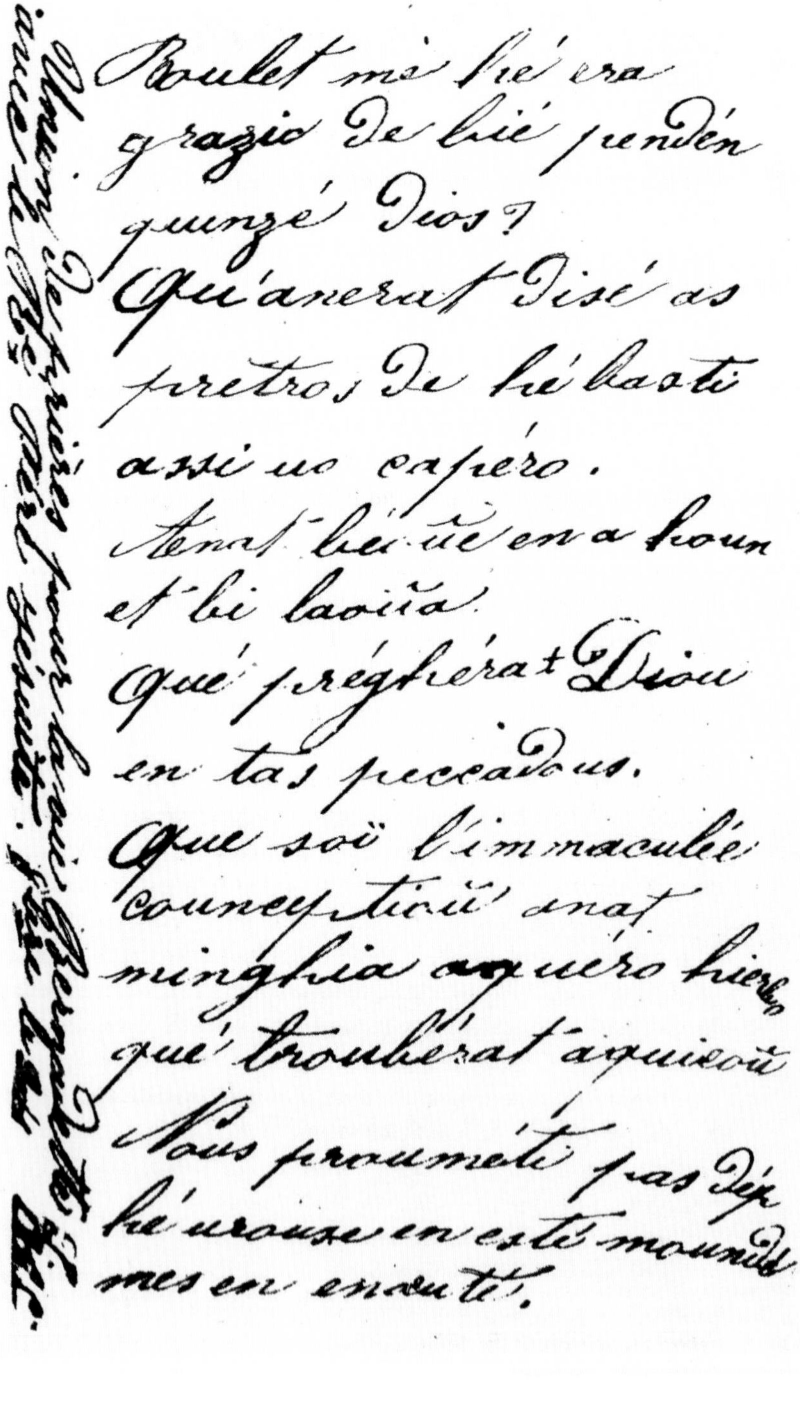

Boulet mé hé era
grazio de bié pendén
quinze dios?
Qu'anerat Disé as
prétros de hé bastí
assí ue capéro.
Aenat béue en a houn
et bi laoüa.
Qué préghérat Diou
en tas peccadous.
Que soï l'immaculée
Councepcioü, anat
minghia aquéro hiers
qué trouberat aquieoü
Nous prouméti pas dép
héurouse en esté mounde
mes en éaoute.

Words of the Virgin transcribed by Bernadette on the back of a picture of St. John Berhmans at the behest of Father Cros.

The words of the Virgin and of Bernadette

We are in possession of three versions of the main words that the Virgin addressed to Bernadette during the apparitions and that contain the message of Lourdes: the autographed version of 24th October 1865 at the back of the holy picture; the version of 12th January 1879 and that of 3rd March 1879. On 31st December 1878 Fr. Cros sent a questionnaire to Bemadette at Nevers concerning the events of Lourdes. Among other things, it contains the French text of the main words pronounced by the Virgin in order to have a further translation of them in the Bigourdan dialect. On 12th January, in fact, Sister Adelaide Dons wrote the words in dialect under dictation from Bernadette and sent them to Cros.

On 3rd March of the same year Bernadette dictated them a second time to Sister Eléonore Cassagnès. The hand writing of this second dictation differs somewhat from the autographed one and from the dictation of 12th January 1879.

What can we say about these versions? Above all, we must state beforehand that both the writing and the pronunciation of the Bigourdan dialect were very difficult and differed from district to district.

Besides, it must be taken into account that the education of Bernadette was at a a very low level. Not only that, but the two versions under dictation were written 20 years after the events.

The memories of Bemadette had weakened.

Finally, her culture and mentality, in contact with the nuns and noted personalities, had become rather French. Both Sister Dons and Sister Cassagnès were not from Bigorre. They tried only to reproduce on paper the speech of Bernadette and then they submitted it to her inspection.

It cannot be said, therefore, that Bernadette gave a precise translation of the "patois" of Our Lady. According to some studies and critics we have, however, the certainty of the authenticity of the words and of their meaning. It is this that counts most for the genuineness and integrity of the message of Lourdes.

Of the three versions, the one that gives most assurance is the autographed one of 24th October 1865. It is the nearest to the events in order of time.

Bernadette still lived in Bigorre and her culture and mentality had not yet undergone the influence of the French of Nevers.

Cros, who corrected and recorrected the text, came from that area and therefore he was the most suitable to reproduce on paper the dialect speech. As regards the main words of the Virgin a critical study has been carried out by the two most important schools of the "Bigourdan patois,,: the Occitane and the Febus.

We will report herewith first of all the version of the Febus school, considered the most faithful.

This will be followed in chronological order by: the autographed one by Bernadette, the transcription by Sister Adelaide Dons.

Third apparition

"The third time I went to the grotto was on the Thursday. I went there in the company of some respectable persons. They had advised me to take with me a sheet of paper, pen and ink and to ask the lady to put into writing anything she wished to ask me."

The "two respectable persons" were Jeanne Marie Milhet and M. Antoinette Peyret. Following advice received during the apparitions, Bernadette offers paper and ink, accompanying this gesture with the following request:

"Boulet avoué la bounta dé mettre vosté noun per escrit?" (Dons)
(Would you be so kind as to put your name in writing?).

The threefold reply of the apparition is as follows:

"N'ey pas necessari!" (Fébus)
(That is not necessary!)

"Boulet aué era gracie de bié t'aci penden quinze dies?" (Fébus)
(Would you have the goodness to come here for fifteen days?)

"Nou ne prouméti pas de hé be (od'esta) unrouse en éste mounde mes en aute" (Fébus)
(I promise you happiness not in this world, but in the next!)

Here is the threefold answer of the apparition. The first answer of the apparition eludes the question of Bernadette by giving a sudden and surprising explanation: "That is not necessary". The second is an invitation addressed with grace and respect: "Would you have the goodness?" Bernadette will speak later about this gesture: "I was astonished! No one had ever treated me with such great respect!

The third answer is a personal message to Bernadette:

"I do not promise you happiness in this world "

It is a forewarning of a life of suffering in illness, opposition, incomprehension and humiliation. Bernadette always remembered this message of Our Lady, above all in the more difficult moments of her life.

And we know how she suffered. How much she paid for her destiny as a messenger of Our Lady. Bernadette did not write the first answer on the back of the holy picture.

Invitation to return to the Grotto:

"Boulet mé hé éra grazio de bié pendén quinzé dios?" (Bernadette)

"Boulet aoué la gracia de bié aci penden quinze dios?" (Dons)

A detail to be pointed out: in the version by Sister Dons Bernadette substitutes the dialect article **ERA** with the French article **LA** that by now had become more familiar to her.

Personal message of suffering:

"Nous prouméti pas dép hé urouse en esté moundé mes es enaouté." (Bernadette)

"Voup proumetti pas d'estre urouso en esta monde ma en l'aouté." (Dons)

Eighth apparition

Bernadette is in an ecstasy. At a certain moment, sadness and joy alternate on her face. She crawls on her knees towards the inside of the grotto, kisses the ground, assumes an attitude of listening. The strangeness of her gestures impresses those present.

The event is reported to the assistant parish priest Fr. Pène by Sister Jacqueline. He invites Bernadette to the Cenac's for the purpose of having an explanation. That same evening she says:

- Today **Aquerò** has pronounced a new word three times: "Penance!"
- She added "Pray to God for sinners" and I have answered: "yes".
- What else has she asked you?
- "She has begged me to go forward towards the foot of the grotto on my knees and kiss the ground as a token of penance for sinners"

Péniténce! Péniténce! Péniténce *(Fébus)*

Penitenço! Penitenço! Penitenço! (Cassagnes)

The transcription by Sister Cassagnès is the only text we have concerning this word.

Invitation to pray for sinners:

"Que pregarat Dìu enta'ts pecadous." (Fébus)

(Pray to God for sinners).

"Qué préghérat Diou en tas peccadous." (Bernadette)

"Que pregaret Diou tas pecadous" (Dons)

"**Que pregarat**" is not an imperative, but a future with an exhortatory and continuing sense. As a consequence, it is not a command but a polite invitation.

This, too, is an exquisite gesture of the Virgin towards Bernadette. It would be better to translate it:

"Will you pray to God for sinners?"

"Anat punà éra terre entà hè peniténce ent'ats pecadous" (Fébus)

(Kiss the ground as a sign of penance for sinners).

This expression is not found in her account at the back of the picture of St. John Berchmans, nor does Bernadette mention it in her various autographed accounts of the apparitions. Many times she speaks about " a prayer for sinners" but never about kissing the ground.

We know, however, from various witnesses present at the grotto that Bernadette repeatedly crawled on her knees and occasionally kissed the ground.

On 25th February in the evening at Cenac's she herself gives an explanation of such a gesture to the assistant parish priest, Fr. Pène:

- Why have you occasionally kissed the ground?
- Aquerò ordered me to do this yesterday as a token of penan for sinners and I promised her so to do it.

Why then has Bernadette ignored this detail both in the transcription at the back of the holy picture and in the various autographed accounts? An oversight? Has she considered it of secondary importance to the message of Lourdes?

I would say rather it was a repetition. She will point out the other gesture similar to this and with the same meaning as regards the message of Lourdes: to eat the herb. She will do this at the ninth apparition. For Bernadette the message of the Lady is important: penance for sinners.

The specific ways are of secondary importance.

Ninth apparition

The message of penance addressed to Bernadette on the occasion of the eight apparition is extended and completed in the ninth.

"One day she told me to go and drink at the fountain and to wash myself. Not seeing it, I went to drink at the river. She said to me that it wasn't there that I had to go and pointed with her finger to show me where the fountain was ....
She also made me eat a herb which was to be found close to the fountain."

"Anat bébe en à hount è by labè." (Fébus)
(Go and drink at the fountain and wash yourself there!)

"Anat béoûe en a houn et bi laoûa." (Bernadette)

The term "hount" corresponds exactly to the Latin word "fons fountain". We know that on 25th February 1858 when the apparition invited Bernadette to drink at the foot of the grotto, no fountain existed. In fact Bernadette says:
"Not seeing it, I went and drank from the river".
Why then did the apparition use the term "hount - fountain" to indicate a spring? In order to give a better idea and to make Bernadette understand. Bernadette was familiar with the idea of a fountain; but certainly not that of a spring. She had gone many times to draw water from the "Fountaine du Porche", not far from her home.
It is improbable that she had seen a spring of water gush out of the ground. Her going instinctively to the river nearby that in someway reproduced the idea of a fountain (flowing water) is evidence of this. If the apparition had told her "spring" (water gushing from an underground well), the girl would have been bewildered.

"Que minyarat d'aquére yèrbe
qui trouberat athéu." (Fébus)
(Eat some of the herb you will find there).

"Anat minghia aquerò hierbo
qué troubérat aquieoû." (Bernadette)

Thirteenth apparition

The thirteenth apparition is characterized by two requests to the priest: the procession-pilgrimage to the grotto and the construction of a chapel-sanctuary on the site of the apparitions.

The requests consist of two terms that in their local meaning extend the message of Lourdes to a universal dimension.

Request for the Procession-Pilgrimage:

"Anat dise ats prètres qu'y bénguen en proucessiou." (Fébus)

(Go and tell the priests to come here in procession).

The request for a procession is well documented by evidence and depositions, but it is difficult to establish its precise formulation . It is missing in the autographed transcription at the back of the picture of St. John Berchmans, as well as in the two dictations transcribed by Sister Dons and Sister Cassagnès. Why?

Frightened by the not at all amiable reception of Fr. Peyramale and confused by his reproaches, Bernadette retained a confused memory of such words. But every time this question was put to her in precise terms she did not hesitate to answer it. On the morning of 2nd March 1858 Bernadette is accompanied by her aunts Basilie and Lucille.

She goes to Fr. Peyramale to refer the wish on the part of the apparition for a procession to the grotto. We report herewith that meeting which so frightened and confused her.

- So what does this lady of yours also want?
- **Aquerò** asks for a procession to go to the grotto.
- A procession to the grotto? But you,re crazy! How do you expect a procession to be held for an unknown person!

The tone of Peyramale is not at all friendly and reassuring. Bernadette is frightened. She is upset. She no longer remembers anything. She is in doubt about everything.

- And when would the lady like this procession?
- Monsieur Curé.. I no longer remember when.
- Are you at least sure she asked for a procession?
- I think so, but...
- Ah, you think so? You aren't sure about it. Well, if one isn't sure of a thing, one stays at home!
- Monsieur Curé.. but.. the lady...
- There are no buts about it! Don't go around pestering people with suppositions. Go home and don't go out again [1].

"I wish a chapel to be built here". View of the three Sanctuaries of Lourdes: the Basilica of Mary Immaculate, the Crypt and the Basilica of the Rosary.

There are at least thirty proofs which witness to the request for a procession.

The word "**proucessiou - procession**" to Lourdes and its neighbourhood means precisely "pilgrimage". It is still used today in this sense. It is seldom considered as a simple religious ceremony. At Bartrès, for example, a village 3 km. from Lourdes, the "Procession to the grotto" is meant as a pilgrimage to Lourdes And the Virgin, speaking to Bernadette in the local dialect, used this term to indicate the local meaning.

Request for a Chapel-Sanctuary:

Anat dise ats prètres de hè
basti aci ue capèro. (Fébus)

(Go and tell the priests to build a chapel here).

Qu'anerât disé as prêtros
de hé basti assi uo capéro. (Bernadette)

In almost every autographed account Bernadette mentions the request for a chapel in these terms: "She ordered me to go and tell the priests to build a chapel on the spot".

In the dialect of the Bigorre and in particular in Lourdes, the expression "as prètros" used by Bernadette was not a common term to indicate the hierarchy, the official authority of the Church. It was, however, more respectful than the other "as currès" used more frequently, but in an ironic and disparaging tone. Certainly Bernadette preferred for the sake of tact a form less commonly used but more respectful.

The word "**caperò**" in the region of Bigorre and in particular in Lourdes does not mean "chapel", "little church", but "sanctuary" "goal of pilgrimages". The "caperò de Bétharram" and the "caperò of Notre Dame de Garaison" were considered as real centres of pilgrimage in the whole region of the Pyrenees. And Bernadette knew them very well, especially Bétharram where she had gone more than once, both before and after the apparitions. Therefore, the two terms "**caperò - proucessiou**" complement each other in the picture of the message transmitted by the Virgin to Bernadette. It is an invitation to the people of God, to the Church pilgrim, to go to Massabielle in a spiritual attitude as pilgrims in order to feel themselves one family.

Therefore, not just a construction as an expression of cult, merely for the carrying out of religious functions; not a procession as a mere ceremony and the expression of an empty and meaningless devotion. But rather a pilgrimage, a strong moment of prayer for the renewal of the spirit; for the change of one's own Christian life. The thirst for a miracle, the hope of obtaining favours, are not the true nor the principal aspect of the message of the Virgin, but rather the expression of one's own self interest. And this thirst for a miracle, above all in the sick, this hope for a favour becomes an affront to Lourdes when it constitutes the only reason for the pilgrimage, if we can call it a pilgrimage at all.

The three secrets

On Thursday, 18th March, Bernadette appears a second time before the Public Prosecutor Dutour.

- Is it true that the apparition transmitted some secrets to you?
- A few days before 14th March she entrusted four of them to me. One of them I have already informed the priests about.
- And in what did it consist?
- In **Aquerò's** wish that a chapel be built at the grotto.
- And the other three?
- As regards the others, **Aquerò** expressly forbade me to reveal them to anyone. In any case, I can reassure you by saying they contain nothing bad. They concern only me [2].

"Que'b deféndi de dise aquerò a persoune" (Fébus)

(I forbid you to reveal this to anyone).

"Quet defendi d'et dire a personne" (Dons)

The text dictated to Sister Dons is almost in the French style. Moreover, the word "**Aquerò** = that one there" is missing. Bernadette speaks about these secrets and the being forbidden to reveal them, in the letter to an unknown person and in the "Grotte de Lourdes", in the following terms: "The Lady also confided to me three secrets, commanding me not to reveal them to anyone".

Sixteenth apparition

The apparition reveals her identity. She signs her message for the world transmitted to Bernadette. She dispels every doubt.

"This time she raised her eyes to heaven, clasped her hands over her breast and told me she was the Immaculate Conception. These are the last words she addressed to me."

"Que soy era lmmaculada Councepciou" (Fébus)
I am the lmmaculate Conception.

"Que soi l'lmmaculée Counceptioû" (Bernadette)

"Que soi l'lmmaculée Conceptioû" (Dons)

Undoubtedly they are the most important words pronounced by the Virgin. An expression which not only enlightens and enhances all the other words, but also gives a meaning to the apparition. It is only right, therefore, that they should have been carefully studied both in their writing and in speech.

Today the form accepted by everyone as the most faithful is the one first reported (that is, by the Febus school). This form was engraved on the pedestal of the little statue sculpted by Febisch of Ly-

FABISCH
QUE SOY
ERA
IMMACULADA COUNCEPCIOU

ons and placed in situ on 4th March 1864 on the exact spot where the Virgin usually appeared and spoke to Bernadette.

Today these words are there as the identification of Lourdes. They are there as a continual invitation to go to the grotto. They are there, as a call to purification, to a change in the spiritual life of every pilgrim who kneels where Bernadette knelt in order to see and listen to Our Lady. They are there as an invitation to innocence and to grace, as a stimulus and as a desire for rebirth.

NOTES

(1) Deposition of Basile Castèrot. Cros, A VIII, page 134, n° 885; page 135, n° 891.

(2) 2nd Interrogation by Dutour. See A. Bernardo: "COSÌ È NATA LOURDES". Turin: LDC Leumann, page 237.

Index

DOUCET PUBLICATION
8, rue Francis Jammes - Tel 05.62.94.27.08
65100 LOURDES
www.editionsdoucet.fr

Photos Editions Doucet
Texts Antonio Bernardo

Printed in Italy by Printaly